WAKE UP

Experiencing your GREATNESS today!

A.J Mata

Published by Aniceto Mata Jr. ©2021

Inquires: www.wakeupgreatness.com

www.thrivewithaj.com | aj@thrivewithaj.com

©2021 Aniceto Mata Jr.

www.wakeupgreatness.com

ISBN: 978-1-09837-743-4

Dedication

Over the years I have had many things shape my beliefs and perspectives. Many of these moments came through my early years. Throughout my life I have also had many family, and friends who God allowed in my life in order to create the stepping stones that led me where I am today, and I am forever grateful for you all.

To my mom, who has always believed in me, even when I did not. To my sister Graze, who has shown me that with enough grit, and determination, anything is possible.

To my younger sister Vanessa, who has reminded me of the power of creativity, and unlimited potential it can bring to this world.

To my brother Josh who has displayed what "truly relentless" looks like and no matter how difficult the challenge, it can be overcome.

To my son Tripp, who reminds me that life is full of adventure and possibilities.

To my daughter Camilla, who has shown me that love for one can grow more and more each day.

To my wife Maxine, who completes the puzzle of the foundation to my success.

Last, but not least, to my father, Aniceto Mata, who is in heaven right now, and who reminds me that I do not need to ask anyone's permission to go after my dreams.

That as long as I believe I can do it, anything in life is possible.

Let your actions speak for themselves. I give all glory and honor to God in all that I do.

I love you all!
A.J

CONTENTS

Preface

We all love a comeback! Why is that? What is so special about the sensation of being down in life, or in a sport, and all of a sudden the tables turn and you come out on top? Is it because of the pride that one gains? Where was all of that pride to begin with?

Now, if you have never personally experienced a comeback, it is possible that you have witnessed a comeback.

It was 2007 and Tom Brady had an undefeated season with the New England Patriots. Everyone figured that they were going to go to the Superbowl and win. All that changed when they played the New York Giants in the playoffs.

Even though it was not one of us in the game, the feeling that transpired during the game sure made it seem as if we were actually one of the players.

Even watching the highlights of that game will automatically bring about those feelings again.

So even if we say we have never personally experienced it, it is fair to say that we have experienced a comeback by the means of being a bystander witnessing it.

Now what is so special, what is so unique about someone being able to turn things around, even when it looked like the world was going against the individual?

What I would like us to explore in this book is how everyone can have a comeback in life. The comeback is what is necessary so that you can take control of your life, figuring out your why, and allowing you to accomplish your true purpose in life. Before doing all this, you must take control of your life.

Having a comeback means you are able to take control of your life!

What happens many times is that we become complacent in life. We try to avoid the struggle so we settle for what is easy. Days and days go by and before we know it, we are stuck working at a job for about 3 years. Then we wonder where the time went? What have we done with our time?

Now, many of us have reached a point where we reflect on our lives and we come to realize that we are left with two decisions. We can either stay where we are, or we can make a change. We can make a comeback!

Out of the two, the easiest change would be to stay where we are—to let life take us where it wants us to go.

Or, we can make the other decision. We can decide to follow our authentic self and make a change for what we really want. So, which one do you think people in the world end up choosing most of the time? Of course, most choose to settle and to avoid pain as this sounds the easiest, and is the direction that many people take.

Why is this so true? When we are watching a bully about to pick a fight, we know what outcome we are hoping for, and what we feel is that we want the little guy to win. So here we are cheering for someone we don't even know, but when it comes to ourselves and the inner battle going on inside of us, we allow the person deep inside to be conquered and defeated by our usual self. The inner self, deep down inside is the little person that wishes they could make a comeback, yet we don't step up.

The secret key is this: ***That person inside of us 'the inner self' just wants us to stop living for other people, and start living for ourselves.*** Yet we constantly year after year allow ourselves to be controlled by our current life situations.

Now, before we make the decision to change, we have to stop and weigh the cost. We know the struggle will be with us the entire way. Therefore, we will ponder the struggle, what it will take and the sacrifices that we will have to make.

As soon as we notice that there is pain, our sympathetic (this is the fight/flight/freeze system that invokes when pain is felt) nervous system will kick in, and naturally prevent us from experiencing the pain. It is not common for us to go through pain. We are wired to avoid pain. But what if both choices bring about pain?

If you choose to stay in the life that you are in right now and are not happy with, you know deep down inside you are struggling to get out and be the person you were always created to be. Even after hearing this you might still decide to keep things the way you are by not making a change. But, ***I can assure you that the pain of regret will always hurt more than the pain that you will feel during the process.***

There it is! Think about it!

Would you rather choose the pain of regret, or would you rather choose the pain you will feel during the change initially? I think that it is easy for me to decide.

I remember when I was making the decision to leave teaching. I had been teaching for about 6 years. I had a secure paying job, and I was about to complete my master's degree. As much as I loved my teaching job, learning, and inspiring my students, I knew that deep down inside I wanted to run my own business. I wanted to be my own boss. I remember one day being out on the football field watching my players practice football, then a question came to me. In the next 5 years, would I be okay seeing myself still being a teacher and a coach? I did not hesitate one bit. I said no. The thought of me not being able to have ever started my business really irked me inside. I could just see myself 5 years from now being very disappointed that I never went after what I wanted to go after.

At the same time, I thought about the decision of making the change. What would my family think? How could I support myself? Do I really have it in me?

The one quote that I kept hearing over and over was, "If you want to take the island you need to burn the boats." —Tony Robbins

I knew that the only way I would be able to make it is if I would be willing to go all in. You'll be surprised how much you will be able to accomplish when the only thing you have depends on yourself to be able to make it in life.

So, the very first thing that we must realize is not so much to reflect on the one-sided choice of whether we should change the trajectory of our life, but that we should look at both paths together.

Was it going to be painful to leave my job of security that I had for six years and open up my own business? Keep in mind, I had just gotten married. Was I willing to use all the money I had saved and the knowledge I had gained to try to make it?

There were months after I left my teaching job that I would break down and cry, wondering if I had made the right choice. I am glad to say that the initial pain I felt when I first opened up my business has gone away. There are still heartaches that arise along the way, but nothing like what I felt the first couple months of taking the leap.

So, stop and ask yourself, *if life is full of pain and struggle, whether you chose to stay in a job that you do not like and regret, or you choose to leave your job and go after what you have always wanted to do and accept going through the initial pain, why not go after the one that gives you biggest reward that you want in the end?*

Either way we are struggling. The only difference is the outcome. On one side you are living a life that you deep down inside did not want to live. The other is what you have always wanted. Both have pain. One just has a greater reward at the end.

Making a change is difficult. It is not easy, but we have to remember **WHY** we are doing what we are doing. This is very important and something we must remember. We must have reasons **WHY** we choose to do the things we are going to do.

There are days some of us choose to go to work not because we enjoy it, but because we know it will provide the food for our family. That is your *WHY!*

Why do some students choose to become doctors, when deep down inside they wanted to be a coach and a teacher? Their **WHY** could have been trying to please their parents who were also doctors.

So, what is your **WHY?**

Before identifying your **WHY,** you must realize the greatness within you. Then you will be brave enough to make the decision and go after what you want by conquering your mind and allowing the peace you need to go after what you have always wanted to go after.

Along this journey you must realize the attributes you have picked up from your family, friends and careers, and how they have given you the tools to help you determine what your **WHY** really is.

When you finally realize your why, it will give birth to discovering your true purpose in life, and this is why I wrote this book. We have to learn to take some time and reflect on things we have never thought about. In order to experience a true comeback, we have to learn to be practical about figuring out what our **WHY** really is in order for us to fulfill our true purpose.

1

The Greatness Within You

Many of us have so many aspirations and goals that we would like to accomplish. The only thing is that we find ourselves constantly talking about what we want to do, but we never take action. It's as if you talk about the greatness that you hope to accomplish, but a year later you are still in the same job. Either nothing has changed or worse, you are further from your goals. You know that deep down inside you were made for something special. There is a reason why you like the things that you do. Defining your goals, writing them and taking action is key. Before doing this, you must believe that you have greatness within you.

Ample research talks about how everyone is unique in their own way. Our fingerprints show proof. You might find someone who has the same number of brothers as you, and likes the same food, but do they also really enjoy going fishing like you?

My younger brother and I have many similar things that we enjoy. Besides working out, playing sports, and having cookouts, he still has other interests that do not interest me. My brother is an introvert and I am more of an extravert. I have no issues talking in front of a big crowd, while he would prefer to maintain a smaller crowd.

The more we study ourselves, the more we see how unique we really are. You might be a morning person who enjoys taking walks in the morning with your dogs. Or, you may not be a morning person, but more of a night owl and prefer to go on midnight jogs. At any rate, it is clear that each person is UNIQUE.

While being unique is something so true, many of us have a difficult time accepting this reality. We try to blend in with the crowd. We want to do what everyone is doing.

Whether it is getting the new iPhone, or it is wearing the type of clothing that is in style, we try to do what everyone else is doing.

The key here is to realize is that your uniqueness is what defines your greatness. In this great big wonderful world, there is only one you. Read that again—ONLY ONE YOU.

I remember growing up, especially in middle school, how the last thing I wanted to do was to be unique. If people ever spotted that we were different, we would hide the things about us that people said were different. How many of you can relate to this?

Little by little growing up, we were constantly reinforced how being different was not a good thing. How there were certain things we had to do to make sure that we fit in. Even when we felt like sharing the unique things that we wanted to do, for the most part, we would hold back out of fear. Fear of being rejected, bullied or alienated.

It's as though there was a voice inside us that wanted to speak to the world, but it never had the chance of coming out. The only person that this voice would speak to was us.

We either found ourselves being a leader that people wanted to follow, or we became the individual that we wanted to follow as a role model. A majority of us just became followers. I would even go on to bet that the leaders had a more difficult time being themselves due to the external pressures of being a leader.

If you were like me, then you were stuck in the middle. You did not want to be a follower, but you found it really difficult to do your own thing—to be you! I remember in high school trying to convince my friends to do something, but I would get these interesting looks. Not to say that my high school friends were not great people to be around, because they honestly were. I still talk to some of them to this day.

But to be honest, I was just the individual who seemed way out there in the sense of always wanting to do something different. One of the things that I was voted for in high school was most outgoing. I am glad to know that I also was voted for the best personality.

I clearly remember coming up with so many different theories and ideas. Many times, my friends would look at me and think, "there he goes again with his thinking". What I really liked about my friends was that no matter how crazy my ideas sounded, they still accepted me no matter what crazy idea I would throw out. I will never forget when I decided to wear a pink shirt that said, "Tough Guys Wear Pink". That's how my thinking would go. Even to this day I laugh at all the ideas I had. Eventually as we grow older, that little voice inside of us gets smaller and smaller. By the time we are close to finishing our teenage years, we are so conditioned to be like everyone else.

What happened to that inner voice? Is it still there? We just have to be still and listen in the silence in order to hear it. We need to bring to light that inner voice. That inner voice reminds us who we really are! It shows us what we really like, what we are really about, and what we would like to do in this world. Sometimes those moments of silence might just reveal to us what we were created to be.

Even though I was able to get some of my ideas out in high school, a vast majority of my ideas and what I wanted to do never got out. Little by little, the voice inside me shrunk, but I am glad to say it did not die!

I clearly remember in college when I had the idea to create shirts to sell them. The idea that I had was that you would take a black shirt and instead of writing the letters C.I.A, the shirt would say C.S.A. It was an idea that I felt would catch people's attention. I will never forget the feeling I felt inside when years later I saw a man I didn't even know wearing one of my shirts.

Since I knew my inner voice stayed there, I continued thinking and having conversations with myself. I believe many of you to this day also still have those conversations when it's quiet and you are alone. This voice inside you right now, that has been silenced, but not shut knows the true you—your unique, authentic self.

Imagine going through your life always wondering what you could have done if you would have let that voice actually talk? If you would have actually made the decision to try something new. Would you currently be where you are right now?

I am here to tell you that even though that voice inside of me was silenced and was conditioned not to speak, I am very grateful I never completely shut out the voice inside of me.

It was that voice inside of me that led me to accomplish everything I have been able to accomplish, and do all the things that I've wanted to do even though I was raised in one of the most economically disadvantaged places in the U.S.

No one in my family had ever gone to college and we lived in a low-income community.

This made the idea of going to college not only less of a priority, but truly a radical dream.

Then, in my freshman year of high school, the voice inside me spoke out for me to attend a university outside of the state of Texas. Focusing on this thought, little by little, it became more and more prevalent in my day-to-day thinking. I would imagine what it would be like to go to a college outside the state of Texas. Even stopping by the high school gear up room and reading all the college pamphlets became a constant thing.

Every time I vocalized what I wanted to do, there was always someone who thought it was crazy! My family thought it was outrageous. It honestly felt that those closest to me would brush off the fact that I wanted to go to a school out of state, and better yet, that I was determined to go.

By listening to the guidance of this inner voice, hard work, persistence, determination, and a desire to succeed, I was able to excel in my academics and be in the top ten percent of my graduating class. (What a nail biter —I graduated number 12 out of 120 students.)

At the end of my senior year, I was accepted to Michigan State University and I received an academic scholarship that would only pay for my first year of college. The remaining years, I had to work multiple jobs in order to pave the way through college for myself. There were times I would have to take the greyhound bus to go home to visit my family. One time it took over 2 days of riding on the bus. There was also a time that I had to spend the night at the airport. At one point I was even working 3 jobs while still taking classes. I am thankful the voice inside me kept speaking out. And more importantly, I am pleased that I made the choice to listen, do something different despite the critics and that I took action! Had I not listened to the voice I probably would have come home after my first year of college, since there was no way I would be able to afford to go to such a big university. Also, this was the same time my parents had decided to get a divorce. As much as I wanted to come home and help my family with everything going on, there was a small voice inside of me that told me to continue going to Michigan State. I mean seriously, it is one thing to get into college, but not a lot of people talk about the struggle one goes through in order to survive and make it through college. From sleeping in the airport one night, to riding the bus for 2 days to make it home, to working 3 jobs at the same time, I am so glad I kept listening to the inner voice.

I will say that the journey I have taken was not an easy one. During this time there were several moments where I just wanted to quit school and go back home. I will say, the pain I was feeling was overlooked by the voice I heard inside. I knew that deep down inside I was meant to graduate from a big University. No matter the current pain I felt, nothing could take away my eyes on the prize. During my time at Michigan State there were so many friendships I picked up on the way, and several life lessons I learned. The lessons have definitely provided guidance for me in what I am doing now. So many times, we are drowning that inner voice that is wanting to come out when in reality they are wanting to come out so that you can meet the friends, and take the career paths that you need to lead you to your destiny. What we keep down is actually wanting to introduce us to the people that we should meet in our lifetime.

Since then, my life has never been the same. I have gone from being the first person in my family to graduate from college earning an undergraduate degree from Michigan State University. I say it with such pride, not because I graduated from the university, because at the same time, there were moments where I could hear myself wanting to throw in the towel, and ignore the small voice inside. The pride comes from the comeback that the little voice inside me encouraged and ultimately won.

Making the decision to go to a big ten university created the building blocks that would lead me to listen to the small voice inside of me. I had gone to college to initially pursue a degree in the medical field. Although I never was interested in blood, and the biology behind it, I found myself taking all of these premedical courses. After my second year of college, I realized how I did not want to be a doctor after all. The only reason I chose that career was so that I could make enough money to help my family financially. I mean let's be real, no one in my family had ever been a doctor. The only thing that everyone knew was that a doctor would make a lot of money. After realizing that I did not want to be a doctor, I made the decision to pursue being a physical therapist. I can honestly say I hated that as well. I remember finishing my internship at a physical therapist office and just could not wait until the end of the day. I could not see myself in a small room working with patients.

All of this changed when one of my friends invited me to attend a Teach for America event that was going to be hosted later that evening. I remember going to that meeting and listening to the speakers. The goal of Teach for America was to get teachers from all across the country and place them in low-income areas in order to help these students compete with other students that came from affluent backgrounds. I recall the speaker talking, and as I was sitting there, I could sense that small voice inside of me begin to rise all over again. It's as if the only person I heard in the auditorium was the speaker talking about Teach for America. What they were about, and how the process worked. I will never forget when the speaker uncovered the map of the United States and how it had a dot on all the low economic areas in the country. As I saw it, I noticed the big red dot in the Rio Grande Valley, in South Texas. This was crazy. That was the place I was from. From there the small voice inside me said, that is where you are supposed to go. I was shocked, but amazed, and intrigued at the same time. How come I had never heard about this.

There I was just thinking about all the students back home, and how many kids like me were waiting for someone to impact their life, so they could be able to do well just like the rest of the students across the United States. As much as I wanted to say, this is what I want to do, this is what I am going to do. I did not. I left the meeting wondering, what would people think? What would my parents think? For the last couple years, the one thing I kept telling everyone was that I was going to be a doctor. Can you imagine what people would think when they would find out that I decided to be a teacher instead? The thought that came to me was that I would be seen as a failure if I decided to be a teacher. I mean, when you compare how much doctors make compared to teachers, there is no question there.

When I got to my dorm, I started wondering what it would look like if I was a teacher. I mean how amazing would it be if I were to be in a position where I could inspire the younger generation to pursue education, and to believe that they could accomplish anything they set their mind on. To be able to tell students that it didn't even matter how much money their parents would make. As long as you have the desire to go, and are willing to put in the hard work, you will be able to accomplish anything you set your mind to. After thinking about it for a couple days and weeks I realized that if I were able to become a doctor, in the end I would be very dissatisfied. I knew that the small voice inside me wanted to be a teacher and work for Teach for America, and inspire the students from my hometown. I came to realize that the only reason I wanted to be a doctor was because of the amount of money that I would be making. The thing was that it was not the amount of money that I would be making, but the financial freedom that I would be able to provide for me and my family.

I remember in college reading the book "Rich Dad Poor Dad" by Robert Kiyosaki. That must have been the first book that I finished with pure enjoyment. I should've realized how much real estate and investments were calling my name way back in high school, but since I never had a family member who did much with investments or real estate, I just brushed it off. Man, I wonder what would have happened if I would have listened to the small voice inside me regarding real estate investment years ago. I wonder where I would be right now.

Eventually, I made the decision that I would no longer be pursuing a career in the medical field, but I would be pursuing a career in the field of education. Now this was not going to be easy being there for the last four years of my life. I had made the decision that I was going to be in the medical field. I knew that this decision was not going to be an easy one. I mean come on, I had no idea what it meant to be a teacher, all I knew was that I wanted to inspire the kids that were back home, and lead them to believe that they could accomplish anything as long as I put the mind to it. I wanted to create students who could have testimonies the same as I have.

And so I made the decision to listen to the small voice once again. I will say there were some very painful moments. It is not easy trying to take a teaching exam that you only spent a couple weeks learning everything that entails regarding being a teacher, and then you have to take the state exam, in order to be certified teacher. I remember going to several different schools trying to get a job being a teacher. Imagine trying to convince the administrators that you were ready to be a teacher, when you had very little knowledge of being a teacher.

By the grace of God, I am very happy to say that I was able to pass my teaching exam on the very first try. To this day, I see it as a miracle.

What are the chances that I chose to listen to a small voice inside of me, and was willing to accept all the pain and challenges that would come from me choosing to leave the medical field and become a teacher? It sure was not easy, but to this day I am very grateful for the choice I made of listening to the small voice inside of me.

Since then, I was able to be a language arts and reading teacher for 6 years. I was also very blessed to coach during this time. I also was able to earn my Master's degree, start my own real estate redevelopment business, become a licensed realtor, and become a real estate broker this year. I am even writing this book! All because I listened to that inner voice, made a decision to listen and then take action on my goals. I'm here to tell you that you can do the same!

It goes in line with what Emmitt Smith, a Hall-of-Famer from the Dallas Cowboys once said, "All men are created equal, some just worked harder in preseason." Or as I liked to say, some just are willing to take the risk and listen to the little voice inside them and go after what they really want to go after.

All I did was continue to work hard and never shut down that inner voice. We all have that inner voice inside us that is wanting to speak out and is constantly silenced. All I did was act on that voice. I think it's time for you to start listening to that voice and acting on that voice moving you towards your goals and dreams.

The moment you start to act on that voice, will be the moment you will begin to give birth to your greatness. In order to create the roots necessary for you to allow your greatness to grow, you must be ready to make a decision. Now before you make the decision you have to be willing to embrace your uniqueness. You must come to the realization that you were made the way you were for a reason. There is a reason you like to eat your cereal a certain way. There is also a reason why you always choose to see the same movies over and over again.

You might get a lot of your co-workers that look at you in a strange way, or some of your closest friends will start to make jokes about what you are trying to do. There is no doubt that this will happen. You have to know and anticipate that people will think that your ideas are crazy, or that you are out of your mind, but no matter what happens you have got to stick with it. *In order for you to stick with it, you have to understand the underlying factor.*

You see, the only reason why what your friends or coworkers say would bother you is that subconsciously you are seeking their validation, and that is what needs to be corrected.

LET'S CORRECT THAT TODAY!

Oh, the liberation and the freedom you will experience when you reach a point in your life where it does not matter to you what people say. Trust me, that day will come. You just have to have faith in yourself and believe that you do have greatness within you.

I remember when I first started my business, it was great getting to know everything about the business. Before I knew it, I found myself a little overwhelmed trying to run my business while at the same time trying to learn how to run a business. I was making sure that I was doing only a good thing by my standards, even though people thought it was a great thing.

Then came the day, where I was tested.

"You are either a smart man, or one of the dumbest people I have met," are the words that echoed from a fellow colleague of mine, when I shared my business idea with him. I remember after meeting with him, it really bothered me inside. Looking back, I can honestly say that even though I said it did not matter what people thought, it really did bother me when they would say that my ideas were crazy.

I mean seriously, who would leave a secure teaching job with guaranteed pay and benefits for something that did not even exist, or that may not be able to provide for me financially? The root of the issue was that I was secretly longing for their validation. I wanted everyone to tell me that the decision that I had made was a brilliant one, but that is actually the opposite of what happened. Every time I shared it, I could feel that people did not know what to say. There were many times when I even questioned if what I was doing was the right thing for me to do. Keep in mind, this was after I had already made the decision to go to Michigan State years back so I had already experienced the critics and doubters then. I would still seek validation from others even after I had demonstrated my success by making the choice to follow my dream and manifest it into the reality of me being a teacher.

The key thing that you must understand before you make the decision to embrace the uniqueness in your life in order to bring out the greatness is that you have to stop seeking the validation of anyone and everyone—especially those closest to you.

Now, it sure sounds simple. But, if you have never chosen this path you will be surprised how much we actually long to be validated in this life and seek people to affirm us.

It's as if we are just waiting for people to compliment the things we wear or the car we drive. What you have to do is put yourself in the position to not care what other people think.

Now this will actually be a lot more difficult to accomplish, because many times we do not even know where we might be longing for someone to validate us.

In order to get to the bottom of this, there is one method of thought that can allow us to see where we long for the affirmation. The biggest indicator of our need for validation will come from people closest to us. So ask yourself, who are the top 10 people in your life right now? You might even be able to list 20. Whatever number that is, you need to get a sheet of paper and write the person's name. After you have written that person's name, the next thing that you will do is rate those individuals on a scale from 1-10 on how much you try to impress those individuals. One being not at all and ten being you live for getting compliments from them.

The people that you try to impress the most or the people that make you feel insecure are the people that you have a tendency to walk on eggshells when they are around.

Now, the issue is not that you are trying to impress them or tiptoe around them. What you have to realize is that the reason you are trying to put your best foot forward is because deep down inside, you are insecure about a certain feature, or attribute about yourself.

I enjoy going to the gym. This is the place where I am able to release a lot of my thoughts, and where I am able to do a lot of my thinking for the business. At the gym, you notice how there are certain individuals that dress a certain way, or even talk a certain way. Sometimes these individuals go above and beyond to put other individuals down by making them feel like they are not lifting a certain amount of weight. What you realize in this situation is that the individual that feels that he has to impress the people he is talking to, or try to bring other people down, deep down inside he is insecure about himself.

For example, you might feel like at work you can never talk about your low economic status because it will let others know that you will never be able to measure up to them. But what you have to do is change your perspective. This is all just the fear of not being accepted. This story is not true but you continue to believe it. *Changing your perspective is the goldmine in your acknowledging who you are and not longing for the affirmation of others.*

One of my best characteristics is that I was always someone who enjoyed talking. Many times when I was in a room, people would be quiet. At first, I found myself thinking that these people probably wanted me to stop talking, or thought that what I was saying was incorrect. Come to find out, there were times when these people were quiet because they were not knowledgeable about the topic on which I was speaking. My perspective went from me not fitting in, to them being the ones who felt like they were not fitting in. This is when a light bulb went on and I began to change my perspective.

The validation that we long for is because of the spotlight that we put on ourselves. The spot light that shows that we are not good enough because when we look at the latest fashion, ours is not as good. That is incorrect my friends. Your fashion is just different. It is unique. It is what the world needs. *So many times, we keep trying to fit into the world, when in reality it is your uniqueness that the world is longing for!*

Instead, what we have to learn is to put the spotlight on the other individual and see the situation in a different perspective. At first it might take a while, but the more you practice it, the better your perspective engine will be running.

Have you ever been at work having a great day, but your coworker just ain't even having it? You are smiling and they are looking at you like you are the last person that they want to see. Then, you try to ask them how they are doing but they don't even acknowledge you. You are left thinking, "Oh wow, I may have offended them because of my smile, or because I was trying to talk to them." *Now this is where you have to stop.*

I love this example that I came up with one day. There was a young man who was in the checkout aisle of the store. As he approached the clerk at the counter, he smiled and said, "How are you doing today?"

The cute girl just looked at him, and rolled her eyes. The young man thought, I wonder what I said wrong? The next couple minutes were filled with silence. There was a girl who was bothered and there was a young man who was wondering what could he have said that bothered the young girl. As the young man paid for his things, he thought he'd give it one more try, and told the girl to have a nice day. The young girl did not even acknowledge him and started attending to the next person behind him. The young man walked away feeling terrible. I wonder what I said? Was it the way I looked? Did I have bad breath? he thought.

It is obvious here that the young man did nothing wrong. For all we know, she was called into work and should have left an hour ago. Yet the young man is so focused on thinking about what he could have said wrong, when in all actuality he said nothing wrong.

It is clear that the young man had no gas in his perspective engine. Now there is a reason why the perspective engine keeps running for some people and for others it is always out of gas. Many times, this has to do with the things we listen to or see on a daily basis. We have so much going on in our mind, better yet our subconscious mind, that we don't realize how much our perspective is being influenced by our own self or by the experiences we choose to let in our minds each and every day.

Remember, the spotlight is not on you! The spotlight should always be on the people that we unexpectedly or expect the validation from. By looking at the scenario of the cash register clerk, we start to think and wonder why she was in a sour mood. Well, there could be many reasons, but the key thing is to put them in the spotlight.

Did the cashier just find out that today was going to be the last day working there because she got accused of something that she didn't even do? Perhaps she was accused by a frequent customer that she provided terrible service just because she was assisting an elderly couple outside loading their things. If the cashier was fired for a complaint from the regular customer, then it does make logical sense why she would not even care to acknowledge what you say. Honestly who would? So you see, there was nothing wrong with the smile of the young man. For all we know, his smile could be the one thing that triggers the thought of a very conniving customer who is just out to get the cashier.

Wow, now that perspective engine is powerful! Not only can you apply this scenario in this situation, but you can also apply the scenario to a variety of situations and people. The most important thing is to maintain your state of being, who you truly are without having anyone influence you. Change that perspective by taking away the attention on you and placing it on the world around you.

Typically, we give our attention to the things that seem out of the ordinary. Now here it is! You have to realize that you are not out of the ordinary, but you are a unique ordinary individual. Everything outside of you is out of the ordinary.

Some of you are probably wondering, okay so I have been a nurse for so long, but have always wanted to be a photographer, and travel the world. There is no way I will be able to make it as a photographer. All my peers will think it is crazy. They just don't pay enough money. What you need to realize is that your longing for a secure job is actually rooted in the fear that you are not going to make it, therefore you aren't fulfilled in your career.

The thing that people have to realize is that your uniqueness is the pathway for you to get what you want in this world. It's the one thing that we need in this world in order for us to experience true fulfillment, yet it is the one thing we keep hidden.

I clearly recall in the movie Dark Knight, where Batman is stuck in a cave. The tunnel scene of the movie is one of the most memorable parts of the movie. If you have not seen it, I suggest you stop reading right now and go on YouTube and play the Dark Knight tunnel scene.

It is a very powerful scene! As the story line goes, Batman keeps attempting to climb the tunnel. Each time he attempts to climb it he wraps the rope around his waist. About halfway through climbing he always falls. TThen there is a part in the scene where one of the captives in the tunnels says, *"the leap to freedom is not about strength."*

So many times, we try to avoid our uniqueness because we think that it will embarrass us, or disappoint those around us. When in reality the only thing you are doing by not embracing your uniqueness is keeping away the freedom and liberation that awaits you. There is so much waiting for you to make that jump and accept who you are. Accept that maybe you weren't supposed to be an attorney and were supposed to go live in Colorado to help that non-profit organization.

As the movie goes on one of the captives says, "fear is why you fail." It is at that moment that Batman realizes what he must do. He must climb the tunnel without the rope. He has decided to accept his fate. At this moment, I recall seeing this scene, and probably feeling like everyone else is thinking, this guy is crazy. Just like people would say to me, "you are crazy for leaving your secure teaching job and opening up your own business when there is no guarantee that you are going to make it"

But you and I must do what the Dark Knight does, before he decides to make the climb, he packs his belongings. He decides to go all in, and then we see him start climbing the tunnel without the rope. As the rising action is taking place in this scene of the movie you can only stop to think, this guy is crazy. Just like everyone will think that your ideas are crazy. Then comes the part in the movie where Batman stops and has to make the jump. This is the climax of the movie; this is where the big decision comes. Right before he is about to make the jump, a cauldron of bats come out, and it looks like they almost knock him down straight to the ground.

Eventually he makes the decision to jump and is able to catch himself on the other side, and climb out of the tunnel.

You see, fear is a liar. It doesn't really exist. The fear that you will experience when you try to embrace your own uniqueness. Your embracing your uniqueness is the key to eliminating the fear that is really not there. It is that uniqueness that will open up the doors to lead us into what we were created to be, and also lead us to fulfill our true purpose. It is our uniqueness that will open up the doors of abundance and success that we so long for, instead of us trying to rely on other things to make things happen for us.

So right now, I need for you to acknowledge as our dear friend Les Brown says, "you have greatness within you". In order to make that greatness come out, you must make the decision that you are no longer going to go through life with a rope wrapped around your waist holding you back from fulfilling what you were really created to do. Now let's make that decision together!

2

The Decision

Now before you change your perspective with all your daily interactions, and accept your uniqueness, know that you will be making a decision. Making a decision is the next step in order for you to make a comeback. In making the decision, it will take a lot of guts. Not a lot of people ever make this decision. What you must know is that there are many people who go through life never making the decision to accept themselves for who they really are. A lot of these people actually stopped living when they were in their mid 20's and received the job that they 'thought' they always wanted.

Keep in mind, 'they thought' they always wanted.

The sad reality is that when they are in their 50's, they will come to realize how they never made the decision to start living for themselves. All their lives they were actually living for someone else. To reach this point in your life now is where you need to be. So are you ready to accept who you really are? Before you can accept who you really are, you must know who you have to become.

The world we live in is filled with so many possibilities.

I think it's the possibilities that exist in the world that keep us from actually deciding who we really are and wondering what we want to become.

Therefore, we let others inadvertently influence our decisions. But that is not going to happen to you anymore. You are completely done with living for other people!

The comeback has officially taken root. You have finally accepted your uniqueness! You must know who you really are and who you have become. The differential between the two is vital. So let me ask you, do you know who you are?

"Yes, yourself".

When reading this, one of you might say, "but, that's crazy because I already know myself. I know what I like, I know who I am, I know what I don't like. There's no way I don't know who I am. If I was not aware of the person, that would not make sense." Then you would go on and on to tell me how you know yourself. In that case, let me ask you a couple questions, and let's focus on every answer you give me.

Do you love your life? No, for real, let me ask you again. If I would give you a million dollars in exchange for your life, would you take the million dollars?
Once again, do you really love your life?
Do you, deep down inside, love your job?
Do you love your marriage?
Do you love the way you look, how you talk, or even how smart you really are?

It is the answers to these questions that will really tell you if you are satisfied with your life. Many times we are led to believe that there are things in this world that will make us happy. We hear about the adventures of money and what it can do for us. Then we decide to invest our time trying to get a job that will give us the opportunity to have a lot of money.

Many of you watch a lot of TV shows that will affect the way you view beauty or what you should have. Whether it's wanting to get a big house, wanting to travel the world, or buying the coolest gadget out there, in reality, it is the things around us that truly have an impact on our life and that lead us to live the life we are currently living.

So are you really where you are supposed to be, and happy where you are currently in life right now? Do you really know who you are? Or are you an influenced individual who is a product of what is around you?

Growing up we all go through so many experiences that shape us. They shape our beliefs, our thoughts, our interest, even the things we do not like. In life there are many things that we value. An example of three things that we may say we value the most are God, family/friends, and work. Yet do we really value these things?

Why is it that we say we value God, but don't really spend time or make time for him?

Why do we say that our family is important, yet our own family members are some of the people that we treat the worst? We treat people that we don't even know better than our family! Then when it comes to work, we spend so much time with work, yet that is the thing that probably brings us the most stress. When it comes to our friends, as much as we appreciate them or love them, sometimes those are the people that let us down.

Why are we confused? Why have we chosen to spend our time and energy on the things that sometimes bring us the most pain? What would life be if we actually really valued the things that we are supposed to value? Why don't we really value the things that we say we value?

What has gone wrong? Why are we in the shoes that we are in? Something has gone wrong with humanity. Something has led us astray. Do we know who we are? Do we know where we want to go in life? Are we so lost and confused that we think we know where we are in life, but yet we do not know? Once again, do you know who you are?

So many things get in the way. From the moment you are born, to when you're a child, a teenager, and even an adult. We constantly get distracted with the things that are in this world. It is these distractions that keep us away from putting us in a place to value the things that we really do value.

Better yet, what are these distractions? We are all different people. My distractions are very different from your distractions. In order to figure out your distractions you have to know who you are in life.

When you figure out who you are in life, you will be able to determine your purpose in life, and that is when you can start making a COMEBACK! NOW YOU WILL LIVE YOUR LIFE, AND FIGURE OUT YOUR PURPOSE.

When you figure out your purpose in life, everything will start lining up. Understanding God, family/friends, and work all of a sudden do become a priority. Yet, not knowing where we are in life is what leads us to all the distractions. So who are you? What is your purpose?

DO NOT LET LIFE CONTROL YOU OR YOUR CIRCUMSTANCES! IT'S TIME YOU START TAKING CONTROL OF YOUR LIFE!

Okay, so now that you have decided to live for yourself. What is the most important thing that matters to you? Now the great thing to know, the decision you are making will release the chains you have been feeling all along in order for you to live yourself.

Remember, the miracles in your life will start happening the moment you start to take action.

That right there is the secret sauce necessary in order for you to make the decision.

TAKE ACTION! Taking action is the key component when you want to accomplish the greatness that is inside of you.

In order for you to accomplish what you were intended to be, you must start by accepting that you will have to make a clear decision about the new journey that you are about to embark on. You have to start by taking the baby steps.

When we look at all the players in the NBA and how athletic they are, we forget to even think about all the hard work, sweat and sacrifice that they had to endure in order for them to get there. We admire their success, but no way do we take time to appreciate the hard work it took for that individual to get there. Why is it that we think it is so easy? What we have got to understand is that no one wakes up being a professional athlete. They wake up having to take action all day every day.

In order to do this, you must set the goals you need to do in order to make a path for yourself. What that means is for you to break down your goals into other smaller goals, and smaller goals so that you can slowly, but surely make your way towards obtaining what you are wanting to obtain.

It is so easy to think that when you imagine what you are wanting to accomplish, it is going to be really difficult. No way, it's just too HARD is probably what you will start to think. What you need to remember is that nothing in this life is hard, it just takes time. Patience is key.

Michael Phelps is a perfect example of this. Many people are amazed as to the success that this individual has been able to achieve. Very few people are aware of all the hard work, or better yet the time it took for him to become the Olympic swimmer that he became. He has clearly stated how he would spend weeks training in Colorado. He would also go to the extent of tracking how much time he was sleeping so that his body would get the right amount of sleep. Notice how in these two scenarios, the hard work is replaced with time. One can state that it was hard work, or as I would like to say, it just took more time.

Many people think it is very hard to build their house with their own hands. To be honest, even an 18 year old kid can build their house with their own 2 hands. They can start by cutting grass on weekends, and saving that money so that they can buy the material they need so that they can start building the wall of their home. They might have to be in the library for the first couple weeks, but eventually they can start building their home. It would not be difficult; it would just take time.

When I first decided to open up my real estate redevelopment company, I had been teaching for about six years. I had only read a lot about investments and redeveloping homes, but I had never actually done anything with real estate investing, or actually ever purchased a property to fix it up. Bill Gates once said, "most people overestimate what they can do in one year, and underestimate what they can do in 10 years". This right here became my mantra. Everyone has their own race they are on. It is not a sprint; it is a marathon that will allow you to experience the fulfillment that you have always craved.

When I started the business, I made the decision that I was not going to be focused on trying to build a real estate investment company right from the start. My primary focus was to learn as much as I could about real estate and investments on top of everything I had already learned. This is another important element you must take with you when you are going to decide to take action. *You must be willing to learn.*

It's crazy to think about it, but within the first 11 months that I opened up my business, I made no money. A person might ask, "did you get anything out of all those months?" What I did earn along the way was the relationships and the knowledge necessary for me to have a solid foundation for my redevelopment company.

What you have to realize is when you are about to enter into a new field, you might have to take some time to learn about the venture which you are about to begin. That is something that some people leave out of the equation. Someone might have a desire to be a great photographer, but they have no idea about the different cameras that exist, or the different angles that a person can take when they are trying to photograph a subject.

Another motto that I live by is the saying, "never an expert, always a learner". This is another thing that you have to be willing to take and embody as you enter into your new profession. You have to be willing to learn as much as you can, and be willing to learn from other individuals who know what you already know but deliver the knowledge from different perspectives and provide different points of view that further your knowledge. You must have a desire to learn about the profession that you are going to pursue. Your knowledge and your uniqueness are what will help create the foundation that you will need to grow your business, or get into the career that you are wanting to get into so that you can be very successful.

Someone might ask, "Are you serious? You were a nurse all these years, and now you're going to spend some time trying to learn to be a photographer?" Well yes, the great thing about it is that now you are actually going to be learning about something that you are excited to do, something that you will love to do, something that you will look back and be very grateful that you took the initiative to take the step to pursue that profession, or that career.

There once were 2 teachers, both of these were from the same high school, and also attended the same university. After attending the university, both of these teachers got hired at the same school they had gone to when they were younger. When both of the teachers got hired, they were both making the same amount of money. After five years, surprisingly one teacher was making $1500 dollars more a month than the other teacher. Why is that? Keep in mind that both teachers worked the same number of hours. Both took the same amount of work days off, and holidays. Can you imagine the teacher's reaction when they found out that their colleague was making $18,000 more a year? They were shocked! How could this be?

The teacher who was making less money, started thinking, I bet the teacher who was making more had put in more hours. To their disappointment, they actually were able to see that the other teacher had worked the same number of hours as he. Since he had not taken the time to ask the teacher how he did it, he decided to ask him. One day during his lunch hour, the teacher who made less money went to the other side of the campus to talk to his colleague. To his surprise, it had been two years since he had actually spent some time talking with this teacher who was making more money.

As he was approaching the classroom, he noticed how students, who seemed to be coming from the office, were going into his class. At first he was confused, but decided to observe what was going on. After seeing several students entering the room, he decided to ask one of the students why he was going into the teacher's room. He let him know that he was there to get the credit for some of the freshmen college courses he would be taking.

College courses? How is it that this teacher was teaching college courses? He then went home and pondered the question. How did this colleague of his start teaching college courses? After work that day he decided to do some research and he was able to find out how teachers could be certified to teach college courses, depending on the specializations that teacher received. He then learned how teachers would get stipends, upon stipends depending on the different specializations that they earned. So guess what happened next?

Yup, you guessed it. He started taking those courses. This teacher started taking the online courses he needed at night, in order to be able to get the specializations. Eventually, after about 2 years this teacher was able to get several specializations. He is actually now making $1800 a month more than he had previously made 2 years ago. 7 years later the same teacher ended up getting hired as principal at the same school he had worked in. This time he was making more than double the salary he had previously made.

So what changed?
Was the teacher working more hours?

The thing we have to realize here is that the teacher gained more valuable skills. When you gain more skills, the world we live in will have to pay you for what you are worth based on the value you can add.

We all get 168 hours a week, nothing more. I constantly hear people say, man if I could get more hours of work, I would make more money. Well, the sad thing about it is that there are only 168 hours every week. As much as we would love more hours, we all get the same time.

What happened here is the miracle that you can also allow to happen in your life. What the teacher was able to realize was that it was not the number of hours that you work that will allow you to make more money, but the more knowledge you gain, the more valuable you become to this world we live in. Oh, how I wished I would have learned and understood this principle when I was younger.

So to tie it in where we are, when you make the decision to accept your unique self and finally decided to do what you have always been wanting to do, you must be willing to understand that it is not hard, it just takes time, and with this decision you must also be willing to learn as much as you can about the profession, or new career you want to go into.

You must empower yourself with the belief that you can accomplish your goals that you set forth. Many times we make our goals too big, and when we see that we are not showing results we get very discouraged. The trick here is to make goals that are attainable. Don't try to stretch yourself too thin. Maybe talk about setting big goals but breaking them down into micro-goals to prove to yourself you can accomplish them and make progress towards the ultimate goal.

After working in real estate and becoming a real estate investor, I've had several people ask me if I could teach them what I am doing. I am always willing to help people reach their goals. Before I decided to show anyone how I do what I do, I always let them know that it is vital for them to get their realtor's license. At first many people will look at me and say, no way, but then there are the few who are willing to take the time and get the realtor license. Although many times there is a temptation to want to take the shortcuts in life, and try to make it up the ladder as fast as you can, this is not from our own nature. It definitely comes from all the success that is shared out in the media, without showing the failures, setbacks, and perseverance that an individual endured to try to get to the top.

The downside with this approach of wanting to get to your goals right away is that along the way we will create cracks in our foundation that will have consequences in future.

Take for example someone who has a goal to lose 50lbs. Their goal is strictly fasting as much as they can. The outcome was that they reached their goal, but deep down at the root of the issue, the problem was never fixed. The person never took the time to change their eating habits. Many times people who lose weight drastically end up gaining the weight back because they never changed their lifestyle, or eating habits.

Hopefully by now I have inspired you to take the initiative to start learning about what has always interested you. One of the best things you can also do is surround yourself with the people who are already doing what you have been wanting to do. It is very powerful to put yourself in the space of the people who are in the career path you desire to be on. You will be surprised by the new insights you will pick up along the way.

So, it is evident that learning is an important factor. During this moment in your life, you will not only be learning about the knowledge that lies in books, but also the wisdom that you will gain through your experiences in life. It is also very important for you to embrace all your experiences and the several types of wisdom that will guide you along the process. Through my years of study, I have found seven pillars of wisdom to be very powerful. Much of this wisdom can only be learned through life's experiences. I hope these pillars of wisdom will help provide you the life guidance you need as you have made the decision to go after what you were created to do.

The first is that of sincerity. Make sure that as you meet people along the way, you develop a character of sincerity in everything that you do. By being sincere, people will help open doors for you that would have been very difficult to open by yourself.

The next pillar of wisdom is that of peace. Try to search for the peace in everything that you are learning, with the people you meet, or the events you go to. There are many people who are in the career that you have always wanted, and their intentions of being there might not be the same as yours.

Thirdly, learn to approach everything with gentleness. Don't jump on something right away. Take some time to see and learn if that is the course you should be taking, or if that is the individual you should be taking advice from.

Next is that of impartiality. As you approach different teachers, always be open to learn from the ones that are different from you. Sometimes these are the individuals that provide different perspectives, and it is the new outlook on things that will help us along the journey of the decision we made.

Approaching everyone and anything we learn with grace is the next pillar of wisdom you should keep in mind. Realize that we do not live in a perfect world, we live in a world where we dwell among imperfect people. Learn to understand that we are learning from broken vases, just like us.

Sixth, be willing to also be patient in your learning. Don't try to rush the learning process, but embrace the learning process. Part of the joy of your reaching and becoming who you were created to be is the journey. Don't let the journey pass on by.

Our last pillar of wisdom, is that of naturalness and freshness. Try to always be careful what you listen to, or those you choose to have around you. Some of the biggest setbacks in life have to deal with the people we surround ourselves with. Always try to surround yourself with those people that believe in you.

Since it is clear that one of the important factors of your decision making is learning, I hope that these pillars of wisdom will help guide and lead you on your path as they have done for me.

Now that you have the tools necessary to make the decision, you know that nothing is hard, it just takes time. Once that belief kicks in, nothing can stop you! Not money, not people, or not even your current limitations. Especially knowing that you are ready to learn everything you can about the profession or career you have always wanted. Now that you have truly accepted your uniqueness, and now that you have made the decision to go after what you want to go after by taking action, you are ready to start tackling the real challenge that will face you!

Facing challenges on a continual basis will be something that you will encounter. In the meantime, there is one enemy that you must be ready for, and not be blindsided by this enemy. This enemy I am talking about is your mind.

Your mind must be defeated! This is the comeback at its peak!

3

Mindset—The Real Bully

Everything you battle with on a daily basis starts with the mind. I have read so many books on the mind, on how it determines where we go in life. I think the one thing people take for granted is the power of their mind.

Scientists have stated that the world's fastest supercomputer requires 24 million watts of power to operate, but our brain only requires 20 watts and operates about 100,000 times faster!

Before we tackle our minds, we have to know that our brain consists of what is called a subconscious mind and a conscious mind. Knowing the difference between the two will allow you to start being aware of what your brain consists of. In order for us to be able to conquer our mindset, you have to realize that you are going to have to erase some things that are inside your brain.

Some of you are probably thinking, get rid of some things in my mind that have always been there? I am telling you with 100% certainty that if you apply what I will show you, you will start rewiring your mind, and in turn start changing your life, and get rid of those thoughts you have always wanted to get rid of. Now this is not going to be something that comes easy, but it is going to take work, and some discipline. Remember, you already made the decision that you were going to make the jump and climb the tunnel without the rope. So, let's embrace the current discipline/pain with open arms.

Believe it or not, your current reality has a lot to do with what's in your mind. We have attracted everything in our life as an outcome of our mind. Many times, we think that our thoughts are in our mind. When in reality, you have to understand that your mind does not really exist. But you're like, "yes it does". Well, I'm here to tell you that your mind does not really exist. It is actually our thoughts that make us think we are living in our minds. You are not living in your minds. You are actually living right here right now. Your reading this book is actually the only thing that is real. Not the thought that you have somewhere you have to go. So realize right now, that there is a difference between your mind, and your thoughts. It is important to remember that if we want to take full control of our mind, we have to be aware that there is our mind, and our thoughts. So before we tackle our thoughts, we have to be able to take control of our minds, and guide them to think how we want them to think in order for us to accomplish what we are trying to accomplish.

Your mind! What a fabulous thing that God has given you. Many times we are unaware that our mind consists of 2 minds. Our subconscious mind, and our conscious mind. The difference between the two is that one mind only functions at around 10% of the time, while our subconscious mind functions at about 90% of the time.

For example, think about when you first started driving a car. When you first got behind the wheel, you were probably overwhelmed with everything you had to do at the same time. Oh, by the way let's always remember to buckle the seat, make sure that no cars are behind us, let's turn on the engine and check that there are no engine lights turned on. This alone seemed like a lot. What followed next was learning how to reverse, while at the same time having your hand on the steering wheel, and your foot on the pedal, keep in mind in order to brake, it was a different pedal. Then as you pressed the gas, you would have to ensure that you weren't over accelerating, all of a sudden take off and hit the car behind you as you were going to reverse. While you are doing all this, you have someone in the passenger seat, talking to you, and asking you if you are good to go. Deep down inside you probably said okay, but between you and me, we were just trying to put up a front that we had everything under control. The last thing we wanted was to show that we did not have control over what we were doing.

So we end up driving. Then we realize that we have to be aware of all the cars that are coming toward our direction. While at the same time making sure I am getting to my location, while at the same time making sure that I am following the speed limit. Wow, can you believe that? It's crazy to think that after all of that, we would continue to learn to drive. Why is it that we continue to learn to drive, even after all that stress of having to do all these things simultaneously?

The interesting thing now, I bet many of us can get into a vehicle and not even think twice about all of the steps we had to go through for us to get to our destination. Just the other day I was driving back home from the gym. When I pulled into the driveway, I didn't even realize that the drive had already finished. I was already home? How fascinating.

The beautiful thing about the mind is that we are able to put our minds on autopilot once we have learned something. This right here is the subconscious mind. The beauty of the subconscious mind is that it is able to allow your body to enter into a state of automatic, where you don't have to go through all the steps you previously had to learn. Think about when you first were learning how to type. At first you were probably thinking, there is no way I am going to be able to learn this. I bet now you are able to type sentences in seconds. Once again, that is our subconscious mind. How beautiful! How amazing that this consists of 90% of our mind.

Well as amazing as it is, I am here to tell you that our subconscious mind can also be our worst enemy. It might actually be one of your worst enemies and you may not have realized it yet. Before we dive into that, let's talk about the conscious mind.

The conscious mind is what we are using to learn at this very moment. When you were learning about the different steps in learning how to drive a car, that was your conscious mind. How amazing that we have a conscious mind that will allow us to pick up new activities that we previously had no motor skills relating to that sport. Keep in mind, this consists of 10% of our mind.

One of you might say, "well if that's the case, I love my subconscious mind, and not so much my conscious mind". Well, what you have to realize is that nothing gets through your subconscious mind unless the conscious mind chooses not to open the door for your subconscious mind. The only reason we are able to eat and talk at the same time, while also holding our new born baby is because we first learned this activity through the conscious mind, which then transferred to our subconscious mind.

So who is the boss now? Hmmm. Even though our subconscious mind allows us to complete 90% of the things we do, our conscious minds are the ones that are really in charge. Now why I am giving you all this explanation you might ask? Well in order for you to be the one to be in charge of your mind, you have to know that your conscious mind is the one in control. Knowing that your conscious mind is the one that is in control will assure you that you are able to take control of your subconscious mind, even though it controls 90% of the things you do. Now this right here is powerful. It is very powerful in that many of us have a debilitating subconscious mind that prevents us from every being successful. This is why this is very important for you to know.

Many of us have been raised through the years and accepted all the negative ideas we have picked up from others and our surroundings. Little by little these ideas became grafted in our subconscious mind. Then years later when we are trying to get a degree, we are unable to because our subconscious mind has been grafted with the thoughts that you will never get a bachelor's degree, because no one in your family has ever done it.

It is one thing for you to accept the fact that you are unique, and have greatness within you, and then be willing to make the decision to change your life. But all of it is worthless if your subconscious mind is the main culprit why you never seem to accomplish your goals. Remember it is that small voice inside you that keeps telling you that you were made to be a professional photographer. So, what is stopping you? It's your mind. To be straightforward with you, it's your subconscious mind. It is your subconscious mind letting you know that you are a failure, that you know nothing about being a photographer, and you don't have it in you.

So, what can you do? Well remember, which part of our mind has the control. Is it our conscious mind that is the one in charge.

You see many times there are people that make the decision to take the step and go after what they have always wanted to go after. The thing is that when they make this decision and decide to take steps towards their goals, they fail because their subconscious mind reminds them that they could never make it happen. When in all reality they can. Especially when that small voice is telling them it is so.

So many times our subconscious mind is controlling us and we do not even realize it. What you have to do is rewrite your subconscious mind. ***The great news is you can actually start rewiring your subconscious mind right now!*** We can do this right here, right now! Let's do this!

What you have to do is get a sheet of paper and write all the negative things you think about yourself. For example, I am too short, I will never be loved, I will not make it, I cannot own a home, I can never be a successful businessman, I can't be a great photographer. You can go a step further and write down some things that are more personal, and you don't share with people, like you are not loveable, you are not loved, you will never get married, you are not beautiful, you are not smart, or you are not good enough. I encourage you to write any negative thing that crosses your mind right now. Remember it is just you and the paper, no one else. You have to write all these things out on a sheet of paper. I encourage you to be honest with yourself even if it is painful.

Okay, did you do it? No seriously, did you take that sheet of paper out and start writing? Remember the miracles in your life will start happening when you begin to take action. So let's do this. Ready, set, go. Take the next 5-10 minutes working on this exercise.

After you write all these negative things, I would like for you to scratch out all the negative things and replace them with all the positive things. For example, if you said, you are not loved, scratch it out, and replace it with I AM LOVED.

If you had a terrible childhood, I encourage you to write it out as a story, but instead of writing all the negative things that happened, I would like for you to write down all of the great things that you would have liked to have happened. For example, if your dad was never there to support you and watch you play at your games, write down that it was always enjoyable when your dad came and watch you play all your games.

This exercise can be very healing as some of you will begin to realize how you actually never heard your father tell you he was proud of you when you were younger, and how you would have loved to hear that. Now you see why you have always tried to overcompensate for things you felt you didn't have. Wow, isn't that crazy? Okay, once you write everything down, the next thing is key. This is where the rewiring of your subconscious mind will start taking place.

With our conscious mind right now, I would like for you to read out loud the different statements of positivity you wrote down. As you are reading them aloud, I would like for you to VISUALIZE yourself in those situations as they are being read. Then, while you are visualizing them, I would like for you to FEEL THE EMOTION that would be taking place. So for example, if you feel you will never be married, I need for you to VISUALIZE yourself being married, and to FEEL yourself getting married. Try to FEEL what being loved FEELS like. The key to it is your FEELINGS OF EMOTIONS and the VISUALIZING happening at the same time. Make the VISUALIZATION as detailed and as specific as you can and really lean into those FEELINGS.

You must go through each line and visualize all the positive things, instead of the negative things. When you do this, you want to really put emotion into it. What you are partially doing right now is rewiring your subconscious mind.

One of the biggest things that I suggest for you to do is remember to actually visualize yourself. VISUALIZING yourself saying, and seeing yourself with all the positive statements.

This is a daily discipline that you must incorporate into your life. Many elite athletes and performers use the art of visualization to mentally rehearse the week or day before a big game or sold-out world tour performance. See it, believe it, achieve it.

It will not be easy at first, as this is something you are not accustomed to. But remember you already made the decision to take the leap of faith and go after what you have always wanted to go after. So start today by visualizing and living through the emotions that you are a successful photographer. As you do this, your consciousness will open the door for all the positivity to enter your subconscious mind. Now, instead of the 10% of your mind being taken over by the 90% of your mind, you can know that the 90% only does what the 10% tells it to do.

You are the 10%!

You are your conscious mind!

You have full control!

It is time for you to take control of your mind! You are the one in charge. Now that you understand that you are able to take control of your mind, know that your mind will be flooded with so many thoughts!

It's the thoughts that seem to fill my mind, you say. Well I have great news to share with you again. Just like you are able to see how you can take control of your mind, you can now also take complete control of your thoughts! Now before we do this, we have to be aware of what thoughts consist of, just like our minds. The only way we were able to start controlling our mind is by being aware that we have a subconscious and conscious mind.

Now it's time to take full control of our thoughts!

OUR THOUGHTS

Every second there are 100,000 chemical reactions taking place in your brain. The one that was very surprising for me to learn was that our minds allow us to experience 70,000 thoughts each day. Can you believe that!?! That's over 2900 thoughts an hour, that's 48 thoughts a minute.

No wonder our brains feel like they never sleep. Our minds are constantly flooding our brain with so many thoughts, things from the past, or even seeing what is happening right before us.

In my life, there have been many years where there were some days I would wake up looking forward to my day. Before I knew it, my day ended up with me being down, or upset. This really led to me wanting to change that.

I did not like how my thoughts would determine the emotions I was feeling. I wanted to be the master of my life. I believe everyone one does. I wanted to write my own story. I was tired of letting my thoughts determine my emotions, especially when the emotions that my thoughts would create were negative.

In order to do this, I spent some time trying to figure out where my thoughts came from. What did this entity, my thoughts consist of? I knew that, if I could determine what my thoughts consisted of, just like my mind, I could in turn master my thoughts. If we really ever want to control our thoughts, we must know what we are dealing with.

That right there is a big key!

You must know and believe that you can go to war with your thoughts. That thought alone can be very empowering. Now the way we can take control of our mind is by knowing what entities our thoughts are made up of. When you know what your thoughts consist of (which is the real enemy we are all dealing with besides our mind. No one ever won a battle against someone they had no clue who they were dealing with). What you have to realize is that the enemy, which is your thoughts, consist of 3 components. That is it my friends!

For the sake of not losing you, I will refer to them as 3 main components.

The first component of your thought is the PRESENT THOUGHT COMPONENT. The PRESENT THOUGHT COMPONENT consists of you being aware of all your physical senses. That being touch, taste, sight, smell, and hearing. Right now you are actually seeing the words on this page. You also might be able to smell the good food that your wife is cooking right now, or the noise that your toddler is making in their bedroom. The PRESENT THOUGHT COMPONENT is actually the one that is the most important and my favorite. It is the thought that actually lets you live in the moment. *When you learn to live in the moment, that's when you can begin to live life to the fullest!*

Your present mind is the peace in your mind that allows you to have a present conversation with the individual in front of you. For example, have you ever been excited to see a friend that you have not seen in a while? You're walking in the store and out of nowhere someone says, "Hey Stacy, how are you?" It is right there and then where you stop and you turn around and you start talking to your friend. The beautiful thing about this is when you are talking to your friend, you are actually living in the moment. You are not concerned about what's going on around you. You are actually engaged in the conversation and everything your friend has to say. So when she shares with you that she just had a child, and just moved into the area where you currently live, you get a sense of joy. You are experiencing true joy and fulfillment during this time. You are not worried about what you have to make for dinner, or what emails you have to reply to. You are actually living in the moment. For the next couple minutes, you enter a state of euphoria, which allows you to live in the moment.

Many of us never get to experience this. How many of us can relate to this example? Your day starts off when you think about the document that has to be turned into your supervisor before you go into work. After contemplating what emails were sent yesterday, you get out of the shower, and get dressed, while still thinking about the email that was never sent out the night before. As you go into your kitchen, you see your wife. She starts saying something about your child's recital and you just nod your head okay. She looks at you, and gives you the stare that you are so familiar with. You look at your wife, and then you say "what?" She says "never mind", and just changes the subject.

At that very moment you start feeling terrible about how you never really take time to actually pay attention to what your wife says. (It's actually called not living in the moment.) While this is happening, you start thinking again about the documents that you forgot to email to your supervisor again. All of a sudden you notice your 2 year old toddler start pulling your hand. He starts telling you "come here dad, I want to show you something." You then tell him "not right now because daddy has to take care of work." You then spend the next 30 minutes at home sending out the emails on the kitchen table while all your family is there. You have no idea what is being said as you are so consumed with work, and getting out those emails. The next thing you know you give all of them a kiss, and start driving on your way to work. As soon as you pull into the parking lot and are willing to go to your office, you start thinking about your kids, and how you so wish you could spend more time with them. You enter your office and you see a family photo. You think about your wife and how you need to start making time for her. Next thing you know you are in the corporate meeting room, thinking about your family.

I think we can all relate to this situation. The Dalai Lama, when asked what surprised him most about humanity said, "Man. Because he sacrifices his health in order to make money. Then he sacrifices money to recuperate his health. And then he is so anxious about the future that he does not enjoy the present; the result being that he does not live in the present or the future; he lives as if he is never going to die, and then dies HAVING NEVER REALLY LIVED."

So how do we learn to live in the present? One of the most practical ways to live in the present is to acknowledge what is in front of you. Here is one practical example.

Imagine that you are inside your brain. Yes, you inside your brain. You are sitting in a room, or better yet you are in the room that you are in right now. Some of you might be at a doctor's office, while others might be reading this book in a car, or in your home office. Either way, what you have to acknowledge is that the four walls around you are the outer layer of your brain. The top ceiling is the top layer of your brain, and the floor is the bottom layer of your brain. Then you have to see yourself as someone who is inside your brain. So for those of you sitting in your car, the doors of your car, the vehicle itself is all the outer layer of your brain. You are the individual that is in your brain. Doing this little meditation practice can be very freeing and allow you to draw out all the noise that is going on around you, and for a couple seconds allow you to live in the moment.

So what happens? Why is it that you can do this practical step to live in the moment, and then all of a sudden you find yourself with so many thoughts going through your mind. What stopped your thrill of living in the moment? Well, I can for sure answer that question, but before I do, I would like for us to focus on the next thinking component. The next thought component that exists is the PLANNING THOUGHT COMPONENT.

I personally love this component of thought as it is the component that has allowed me to accomplish a lot of things that I have been able to accomplish. The PLANNING THOUGHT COMPONENT of the mind is something that has brought out a lot of the new ideas of me wanting to start my business, wanting to start a Shirt business, and even writing this book.

Making the decision to become a professional photographer and travel the world definitely requires some planning. Each of us while trying to earn a degree meet with an advisor and the advisor creates a career path for us to follow. This is what I call the PLANNING ENTITY THOUGHT. It is our very good friend.

When you decide to choose a new path in life, it is going to require the planning necessary for you to create the pathway necessary for you to reach those goals. That is where the PLANNING THOUGHT

COMPONENT kicks in. Before you know it, you take out your journal and start journaling the next steps you are going to take. From meeting with the advisor, to meeting with someone in that profession, all of this is the planning.

A lot of us never carry a journal, or a notepad in order for us to give growth to the PLANNING THOUGHT COMPONENT. If you want to be someone who is able to take control of their thoughts, then I suggest that you buy yourself a journal or notebook. Your PLANNING THOUGHT COMPONENT needs to be nurtured and attended. The way you can assist in this is by buying a journal, and taking it wherever you go. I guess now you know where all of the million-dollar ideas came from.

Man, how I wished I would have known this concept sooner. The great thing is you can be practical about this and buy a notebook today and give way to your PLANNING THOUGHT COMPONENT. Now, some of you may have access to a notebook right now at this very moment. I suggest you put this book down, and get that notebook and start writing your ideas! Start planning the necessary steps you will need to take to reach your goal. Come on. Ready, Set, Go!

Okay, so now how did that feel? I bet that felt great! The reason why is because you are giving the nutrients that your PLANNING THOUGHT COMPONENT needs. Now I bet for some the planning was easy. And for others, I bet you found it a little difficult. Before you knew it, you were thinking about something you did not do, or something else that had to get done. To be clear with you, you were not living in the moment. Focusing your attention to the present is key.

So there you go, when you want to live in the moment, you put your PRESENT THOUGHT COMPONENT to use, and before you know it you are distracted by these other thoughts that keep entering your head. Then when you decide to enter your PLANNING THOUGHT COMPONENT, you are good for a while, and then before you know it you spend half the time on thoughts that don't relate to nothing you were planning on.

It sounds useless. You might feel defeated. Well I am here to tell you that there is another thought component, and it is this thought component that keeps getting in the way of your living in the moment, and your planning your way to success. This thought component is what is called your PRATER/CHATTER THOUGHT COMPONENT. It is taking the time to understand what the PRATER/CHATTER THOUGHT COMPONENT consists of.

Now this component of your mind is the one that I want to focus on. Many doctors and psychologists have different names for this type of entity in your mind. I like the word PRATER as the clear definition of prater is a person who talks foolishly, idly, or at tedious length. The PRATER/CHATTER THOUGHT COMPONENT is the thought component that we really need to understand how it works. Once we understand how it works, we will need to clarify our beliefs system so that we can ensure that we do not let this thought component get in the way.

The PRATER/CHATER THOUGHT COMPONENT, unlike the PRESENT and the PLANNING thought components which help us live in the moment, and plan our way to success, it is the thought components that takes it all away.

For example, I previously had someone call me about an issue regarding a house that I sold. They told me that they recently had a hurricane pass the home, and water entered through the home. When I heard this information I was shocked. The reason I was caught by surprise was that, before purchasing this home I inspected the home and it had no issues to show that water had ever gone in the home, or that water would go inside the home. Even after I inspected the home everything checked out perfectly. We were able to see that the house had no issues previously of water ever entering in the home. After I spoke to the individual and explained to him the situation, after getting off the phone, I will say that deep down inside I started feeling a sense of failure within me.

The surprising thing about it is that the next couple days I still felt like I had a heavy burden in my heart. I could not get this heavy burden out. I know that the emotions that I was feeling were due to the thoughts, the PRATER/CHATTER THOUGHT COMPONENT, that were overtaking me. As time went on, I would be in the PRESENT THOUGHT COMPONENT, and the PLANNING THOUGHT COMPONENT, but as soon as I thought about the house situation and how water had gotten into the home, I felt miserable again. It's like I could not escape this trap. I would get so frustrated. Especially when I spent the next hour having lunch with someone I was really looking forward to and now, all I would think about is that whole situation of water getting into the home.

Each and every one of us has several thoughts that go through our mind throughout the day. What you have to realize is that they either come from one of three components, your PRESENT, your PLANNING, or your PRATER/CHATTER thought components.

When a chatter thought enters our mind, we are prone to do a couple things which include evaluating ourselves, comparing ourselves, or judging ourselves. For the sake simplifying the wording, I will refer to the PRATER/CHATTER THOUGHT component as delivering the ECJ--meaning we are either evaluating, comparing, or judging the PRATER/CHATER thought that has entered in our heads.

Keep in mind we have several thousand thoughts that enter our minds. Are you seriously telling me that you have control of every thought that goes into your head? Let me be clear with you right now, not every thought that enters your mind is your thought. Let me say that again. Not every thought that enters your mind is your thought. When you have been watching horror movies, the crazy thoughts that might cross your mind are not your thoughts. Many times it is just your brain that is delivering images that have been seen and combining those with images that you were already aware of.

The way this PRATER/CHATTER THOUGHT COMPONENT works is that it naturally loves to attend to all the thoughts that pop into your head. Then it will deliver the ECJ, (evaluator, comparison, judgement) or where you fall in regards to that thought. The outcome of that situation will leave you feeling so many negative emotions.

Typically, we are the individuals that bring ourselves down and don't even realize it. What I need for you to do is to be aware that there is nothing you can do to control the situations that happen in life. You can only control how you respond to them.

This PRATER/CHATTER thought component loves the ECJ. Take for example the situation that I laid before you. Without me realizing it, I would wake up every day and have a thought about how I sold this individual a house that allowed water to come in and that I had no control over this. As soon as I thought about that, right away I would analyze the thought, and without even realizing it I would evaluate myself as a terrible redeveloper. I was doing this without even being aware of it! Self-awareness is critical.

This in turn would lead me to feel the emotions that I did. It is this point exactly that I want you all to see, and I need you to understand. We all have what I call chats or thoughts raising in our head. We need to realize that a lot of the thoughts that take place are not our thoughts. Many times, when these thoughts are in our head, we tend to evaluate ourselves, we compare ourselves, or we become the judges of the thoughts that we are having. This just leads to us feeling terrible.

For example, many women in today's society have a very low self-esteem. One possible reason for that is because whenever they get a PRATER/CHATER thought in their mind, they compare themselves to see if they look as good as the celebrity women that we see on TV. Now we all know that a lot of the photos of women in the magazines are photoshopped, especially when today's technology makes it so easy.

What these women need to do in order to get rid of those thoughts and feelings is to stop being the evaluator, or the person who is comparing the way she looks with another woman. What she needs to do is believe that she is a beautiful woman. She needs to believe that there is nothing that she can do to control what happens on this earth other than choose how she responds to life situations. She needs to know and understand that everything on this earth happens for our benefit, even when it doesn't look like it, it is for our benefit. This is very much tied to our belief systems. This is the next topic of conversation that I want to focus on. In order for us to master our chatter thoughts, we need to have a solid belief system.

Before I move to the next chapter, I do want to say that many of us have several threads of chatter that keep going in our minds. We need to stop evaluating, stop comparing, and stop being the judge of those chatter thoughts. Many times these chatter thoughts are not even our thoughts. They might be ideas or thoughts from movies that we've seen. As soon as we get that thought, we need to not even acknowledge those thoughts by judging ourselves in that time, by comparing ourselves to the thought presented, or by evaluating ourselves in those thoughts.

When you realize that it's your chatter thoughts that get into the way of your present and planning thoughts, then the questions are "okay, how do I get rid of my chatter thoughts? Can I really get rid of my chatter thoughts?" I am here to tell you that it is possible. You no longer have to be someone who is not able to live in the moment, or someone who has a difficult time planning their life of what they are wanting to do, or where they are wanting to go. Now you will be someone who is able to give birth and growth to your present and planning thoughts, and put down your chatter thoughts that consume you each and every day.

The way to do this is that you must destroy the PRATER/CHATTER THOUGHT COMPONENT once and for all. I am here to tell you that you can do this! The first step in doing this is making sure your belief system is where it needs to be.

You have to also realize that most of us have lived in a negative world for most of our life. If you turn on the television today, you will easily see all the negative things going on in the world. This has given more food to our PRATER/CHATTER THOUGHT COMPONENT of leading us to evaluate, compare, and judge ourselves in a negative way. I think it's time to put a stop to this once and for all. But first we must make sure that our belief system carries the right foundation for us to destroy this PRATER/CHATTER THOUGHT COMPONENT that has so taken over our lives.

4

Our Beliefs—Establishing PEACE

Our beliefs are something that we are raised with. Many of us are raised to believe that we have to go to church and believe that there is a God. While others may never take the time to go to church or have a belief in God. Our belief is also based on what we think is right and what we do not think is right. Some of us have been taught that the only way to go somewhere in life is by working hard. While others have never really been taught the philosophy of what it means to work hard. Sometimes the only way one can be taught the essence of hard work is by going through it yourself.

Either way, a lot of times what we believe is influenced by the world around us. There are those that are the exception and have studied another religion and chosen to leave their beliefs and taken on a new belief system. As for many of us, we believe what we have been raised to believe and these beliefs end up shaping the way we end up seeing the world, and how we end up living.

I was raised in a home where I was taught to always respect my elders. Even in middle school or high school, I would never even think about raising my voice to a teacher. If I ever did this, I probably would not eat for a week or be able to sit on my butt for a whole week. When I was a teacher, I was shocked to see how many students would disrespect their teachers. Much of this comes from the home, and is taught.

Sometimes it does come from the peers we are raised with and surround ourselves with. But, if a parent makes a distinct effort to instill into their kids that one of their values is respect, that should stay with their child even when the parent is not in the same room as the kid.

Our belief systems are constantly being changed, but it comes from our roots. Growing up, my parents never really taught me the importance of being financially stable. This had a negative effect on me and when I went to college. I recall taking several loans to make ends meet. On top of that, I remember taking out a loan for a car that I should have probably only spent half the amount of money. Because of these careless mistakes, I racked up so much college debt--especially with having to pay out of pocket for four more years after my first year.

It wasn't until after I graduated from college that I realized how important it was for me to be financially stable. In order for me to be financially stable, I would have to learn what it meant to be financially stable. This took a couple of years, but after listening to a lot of the Dave Ramsey podcast, it shaped the way I viewed my finances. I soon found myself not spending money the way I thought to spend money. I realized that instead of spending money, I would use it so that I could pay off my debt. I learned that there was no need for me to live beyond my means, but that I could live with only 70% of my paycheck or less.

I do remember when I first got paid, my father had a really difficult time understanding what I was trying to tell him about avoiding debt. He had the belief system that we should enjoy each day and how everyone needs to get into debt in order to enjoy life. I, on the other hand, had a different belief that I was able to pick up after college. The reason for that was because I wanted to start saving money so that I could pay off my debts and then be able to invest or one day open a business. Then I would be able to make money and provide the financial freedom for me and my family.

My financial struggle is just one concept of certain beliefs. There are many other beliefs that impact the way we live. For example, another one of those concepts is that of love. If growing up you were never shown a lot of love from your mom or your dad, you probably found yourself longing for that affection from others. But if you were raised with loving parents, many times your focus was not based on trying to find someone who loved you. Your focus was on other things like trying to go to college, or learning about different things. This is very clear in my little sister, in that she was the youngest one in the family and we constantly showered her with love. Her thoughts with regard to love when she was in middle school were very different and unlike her high school friends who had many boyfriends.

She eventually started dating a boy and is still dating him today. Her taking a while to choose a boyfriend her senior year had a lot to do with the love we would show her, so that she would not long to get that love from somewhere else. Even though it took her a while to finally start dating a boy, I can attest to the fact that I played a huge role in sharing with her my beliefs about relationships when she was younger. It does not surprise me that she is still dating the same boy she started dating at the end of her senior year. Even after dating him for a couple of years now, she is still certain that she is not ready to get married. This is different, unlike some of her friends who have already gotten married. It's definitely the values that were instilled in her.

When she was in middle school, she and I spent so much time together. During our drives in my truck, I would ask her how school was and I'd also ask her about boys. It was here where I would explain to her how saving herself for one guy was the best thing that she could do. That she needed to trust that there was a God who had a special someone waiting for her.

It is evident to see how our belief systems shape and impact our lives. But the question that we must continue to ask ourselves is, if our belief system impacts us on how we see the world, do we all carry the same belief system or is it different? In order to answer this heavy question, we must look deep down inside and see what we really believe and if our belief system is the same or different. *If our belief system is the same then each and every one of us can have the foundation of our belief system in place to be able to help us destroy the chatter thoughts that cross our minds.*

There's so much knowledge out there that talks about the different things that created the earth, or whether or not there is a God. For me, I can honestly tell you that I believe that there is a God. I can only share this from the personal experience that I have gone through in my life. When I think about a boy who left his family to go to college with no money and was able to make ends meet, it blows my mind how I was able to get through college without any financial assistance from my family. Keep in mind, I went to a college that was over 1500 miles away from home. During college is where my relationship with God grew. I learned in college that Jesus Christ came to earth and died on the cross for my sins. There was nothing I needed to do to earn God's love, but that God's love was there for me because of what Jesus Christ did for me on the cross. I then put my faith in Jesus Christ. Since then, I can say I have been walking with the Lord the last 15 years of my life. It is crazy to think where the time has gone. It is clear to me now that it has not been the destination, but the journey that has been the biggest blessing for me.

Both in college and after college, I have met many people who have had several different beliefs than myself. Some were Hindu, Muslim, Catholics, atheist, agnostic, etc. Even though we all believe in different things, one thing has been clear to me is that each and every one of us longs to figure out what is the meaning to life. Or is there meaning to life?

I believe that deep down inside of us each and every one of us longs to know whether or not there is meaning in life. For this is the reason early in my life, I took the initiative to truly figure out what was the meaning in life. Research shows that each and every one of us has desires. We have an innate desire to eat so it is completed with there being food.

We have an innate desire to be physically intimate with another person, so it is met with us being physically intimate with another person. I believe that meaning in life has to be met with something that has meaning.

Can you imagine being in a room that is completely dark? Well, how you know that you are in a dark room is because you are aware of the light. If only darkness existed, you would not even be able to tell that you are in a dark room. The only reason why you know you are in a dark room is because of the absence of light. Since there is no light, you know you are in a dark room.

For me as a child, as long as I can recall, I have always had an empty feeling inside. This feeling inside me became meaningless since I had no idea what meaning was inside of me. Because of this I came to the conclusion that there must be meaning on this earth. There must be a way and a truth that exists out there. The way and the truth for me truly started in college.

I had attended a retreat where I heard this guy tell me that there was nothing I needed to do to earn God's love. God's love for me was sufficient, because he has sent his son Jesus Christ to come die on the cross for my sins. This in turn allowed me to have a relationship with God. God would accept me as the person that I was. Man did I feel so much peace come upon me.

The interesting thing that I have found very fascinating is that the Christian faith is the only faith that exists in the world today that says there is nothing you have to do to earn your ticket to heaven, it is a free gift, not by works.

As I tried to grow more knowledgeable, I came to see how the people who had no faith in God had even greater faith than me. To have no religion is a religion in itself. To have faith in nothing, is to have faith that there is nothing. So for anyone who has never believed in God, I give them my respect because it takes a lot more faith to believe that there is no God. As for me, I do believe that there is a God. I do believe that when I die, I am going to heaven. I do believe that there is eternal life. Once again, I can only say that I believe in these things because of the experiences that I've gone through.

Some of you may even question the Bible. Some of you might even question my experiences, but whether you believe in God, or don't believe in God, the truth lies in the fact that we all have a belief system. Even though my belief system may be different than yours, it is still grounded with the same foundation.

Now the key point I am trying to make here is that we all have faith in something. Some of us have faith that we are loved by God, others have faith that there is no God, and it is an illusion. The person that has no faith and thinks that God is an illusion, has chosen that belief, and therefore they have PEACE about it. In the end, both sides have made the decision and long for that PEACE. It is a belief system that is grounded in PEACE that connects us to have the same foundation.

So if our decision on faith is based on PEACE, it is fair to say that our foundation in our beliefs must be founded on PEACE.

Evolution has played itself out to believe that all things are created, which have led to other things being created. Therefore animals evolved into humans, etc. They have peace about the evolution of man. Their belief is still grounded on the PEACE that they feel inside, based on that decision.

For those that don't believe in God, I would ask, would God create something he did not love? Imagine creating a game that you hated and playing that game every single day. I would tell you that I would personally get rid of that game on the very first day. Therefore, it is safe to say that if there is a God, and we have been living on this earth for thousands of years, he must enjoy us. I would go further and say that if there is a God, he loves us with such unconditional love. It is right here where there is PEACE. If not, then you have PEACE that there is no God. Either way PEACE is still there.

When you are in an accident, and need to have surgery, and are unable to go to a state playoff game, there is no peace in knowing that you missed out on the state playoff game. Yet our belief system is grounded on faith that there is a God and everything happens for a reason. This right here gives us PEACE.

So whether you believe in God, or don't believe in God, our beliefs are grounded on seeking the PEACE we all long for. Whether you have peace that there is a God or have peace that there is no God. The peace you long for is what creates our faith in what we believe. If peace is what matters to you, then our belief system must always be built on the foundation of PEACE.

Now this is where I would like to tie in the PRATER/CHATTER THOUGHT COMPONENT. When we have all of these chatter thoughts running through our head, typically there is no PEACE, especially when you keep evaluating yourself, not meeting a standard, or comparing yourself, and even judging yourself that you have failed.

This peace is easily taken away with all the negative things we see in the world--especially the media. The media constantly shows all the negativity that is going on in the world. This can destroy our peace if we let it. Some of us don't even have that peace anymore. Yet, it is the longing for peace that helped create our faith in our current belief system.

You need to get that peace back!

Let me be clear with you right now. Some of you are living in your chatter thoughts, and you should not be there. If each of our belief systems are grounded on peace, then the outcome of your chatter thought should give you that peace. Whenever a chatter thought enters your mind, you need to acknowledge the fact that everything happens for a reason. The reason it will be very difficult for you to get the chatter thoughts out of your head, and keep them from taking away the peace that you so desire is because as soon as you get a chatter thought, you take on the evaluator, the comparison, or the judge and you feed it with so much negativity.

Yup, you're not good enough. Yup, there is no reason to invest money because the economy is doing terrible. Now where do you think all of this comes from? You're right, the media.

Some of you might have to take some time and get away from social media, the news, and even television. You need to start surrounding yourself with positive things. I have had moments in my life where I have had to fast from social media, the news, and negative movies. If you have not done this, I encourage you to start with 1 day, then 3 days, then a week, then 40 days, ½ a year, or even one year.

The changes you will start seeing in your life will be monumental when you stop letting social media consume your life. That is a topic for another book, but you need to be aware of all the negative news and inputs you're listening to on a daily basis.

The key here is to realize that our belief systems are what we can use to control our chatter thoughts. We must realize that when we become the evaluators of our life, compare ourselves to other people, or even judge ourselves, we will be more inclined to look at ourselves in a negative way because of all the noise we hear. When we finally take some time to draw out the noise, we can be more aware when the chatter thoughts cross our heads. Then we can get away from being an evaluator, a comparer, or a judge, and acknowledge the fact that we have no control with things that happen. Everything happens for a reason. As soon as we acknowledge this, we are able to get rid of the chatter thought entity that tries to dominate your mind. We can finally kill the enemy and take control of our mind. In reality we are the one with the true control. We can either get the peace we are longing for, or take away the peace we are longing for. When a chatter thought crosses your head, you need to not acknowledge that thought. Whatever you do, do not compare yourself, evaluate yourself, or be the judge breathing condemnation down your throat.

Your belief system was created with the foundation of PEACE. Therefore, we must do whatever we can to maintain that peace. When you start doing this you will begin to destroy the PRATER/CHATTER THOUGHT COMPONENT and give more growing to your PRESENT

THOUGHT COMPONENT and PLANNING THOUGHT COMPONENT. How does that sound?!

After being a teacher for six years, there were times when I would think if I wasted all that time, since now I am running a business and going on my sixth year. Can you imagine where you would be if you would have started the business a long time ago? I would have had over 10 years of running my own business. Man, did I really waste those years in the chatter thought that would try to invade my way of thinking.

There I was trying to evaluate myself in a negative way. Here are 3 practical statements you can tell yourself when you notice a chatter thought entering your mind.

1. Everything happens for a reason

2. There is nothing you can do to change the past

3. Don't even acknowledge the thought by evaluating, comparing, or judging.

If you feel you messed up with choosing the wrong career in your life, quit being the judge, and realize that God allowed you to meet all those people for a reason. They are the people that have brought joy and meaning to your life. Or, they are the type of people you have realized you do not want to be around. Either way, the main goal we have to accomplish is to seek and find that peace. The way we get it is by the acknowledgement that everything happens the way it does, just like evolution states, or our belief that God is in control and everything happens for our own good.

In order to take control of our minds, we need to make sure that we affirm any thought that crossed our mind in order to get the outcome of peace. Also, we must acknowledge the fact that some thoughts are not our thoughts. Quit being the ECJ (evaluator, comparer, judger) of those thoughts. Take a step back.

Our beliefs are grounded on peace. That peace is essential in destroying the chatter thought entity that tries to take control of our mind. When we destroy this chatter thought entity, we then give more birth and growth to our present thought, and planning thoughts. We need to acknowledge that everything happens for a reason. That we do not have control, and since our beliefs are grounded on peace we need to affirm and acknowledge it. When we do this, we destroy the ECJ, and therefore destroy the chatter thoughts that we get stuck in our heads and that have been there for years on repeat most of our life.

Wow, now that is freeing! We have now been given the tools to destroy the chatter way of thinking. When we do this, we will give ourselves more time in planning our way to success and the best of all, living in the moment!

If you are someone who has never taken the time to destroy your chatter thoughts, it has led to 2 monsters that many people struggle with today. These 2 monsters are that of depression and anxiety. The chatter thought entity is one of the main reasons many of us have dealt with depression and anxiety. Part of your longing for that peace is the secret tool you will need to get rid of the depression or anxiety you have been dealing with.

When you search for that peace, it will allow you to destroy the chatter thoughts. This in turn will start the process of holistically getting rid of any depression or anxiety you have dealt with.

Before you tackle depression and anxiety, you must know from where they are rooted. The chatter entity is one of the main reasons why we have dealt with depression or anxiety. When a chatter thought enters our mind, the ECJ is what creates all the anxiety and depression. Anxiety is rooted from the fact that we are unsure of what is going to happen in the future.

Some of the chatter may be that of doubt, wondering will you have enough money to make it through the week? Or worry, will your kids meet the right friends? Will you be able to make the team? All of this is the PRATER going on. Useless chatter as I like to call it. What you need to do is to realize that there is nothing you can do to control the future. For myself, I believe that God has everything under control. I am supposed to get the home to fix it up and the seller will accept my offer. If I counter on a property and the person decides to back away, I trust God will work everything out for me. As one of my favorite verses in the bible says, 'And we know that in all things God works for the good of those who love him, who have been called according to his purpose' - Romans 8:28. For me I am glad that I have a bible that gives me all the peace that I need.

Remember, when the emotions of peace arise, it is there where you have destroyed the power of the chatter thought entity. You can accept that fact that if you did not make the team it wasn't meant to be.

I remember when I first got my teaching job, I was shocked that I was going to be assigned to be a reading and language arts teacher. Now one thing about me is that I love science, and I have always loved math. My weak subject had always been reading and language arts. You know I will say that when I first got to the job, feelings of anxiety would want to rise up. Then I remembered that the good Lord works everything good for me. So, I accepted a teaching job. Not that I would not have accepted it, because I would have accepted any teaching job at that point in my life. I am glad to say that because I was an English Language Arts teacher, the Art teacher was placed a couple doors down from me. If it wasn't for that reason alone, she would have never introduced me to my wife. Oh, how crazy to think about the fact that the teaching subject that I did not want to do was the subject that would eventually lead me to meet the woman I would later call my wife and would spend my entire life with.

Can you imagine if I would have let the anxiety get a hold of me? I would have probably never made time to get to know my co-worker who introduced me to my wife. Instead of seeing a teacher who was willing to not let the uncertainty of the future get in the way, she would have seen a worried teacher. Imagine what my wife would have thought when they told her how there is this teacher who does not seem to be happy with his job, and is always worried. Years later I came to find out that the one thing that my coworker told her about me was that I loved my job. Better yet, I was willing to accept the fact that I had no control of the future, and I was going to enjoy the process along the way.

That's what a lot of you have to do. You have to accept the idea that there is nothing you can do to control the future. Remember life does not happen to us, but it happens for us.

Say it with me, LIFE DOES NOT HAPPEN TO ME --LIFE HAPPENS FOR ME!

Every time a chatter thought regarding the future crosses your head, remember to accept any outcome that may come and acknowledge that everything is happening for your own good.

Now as far as depression, the same rule applies. The only thing different with depression is that, unlike anxiety that deals with the future, depression deals with the thoughts of your past. Many times, you will have thoughts of failure that cross your mind, or how you should have never dated that person, or taken that job. What a failure you must be, right? Wrong, YOU ARE NOT A FAILURE. FAILURE IS JUST ONE STEPPING STONE CLOSER IN YOU GETTING WHAT YOU ARE AFTER. For me something that has helped me along the process of avoiding getting into the states of depression is the acknowledgement again, that whatever happened in the past happened for a reason. Maybe dating the person was necessary so that you could figure out what you really do want in a husband or what you don't want in a wife. Maybe the reason you worked at a job that you hated so much was to show you that whenever you become a boss you will never degrade your employees, but you would lift them up and try to understand what they are going through.

For me, something that helps me find the peace is another verse in the bible which states, "For God did not send his Son into the world to condemn the world, but to save the world through him." -John 3:17. How amazing it is for me to know that there is no condemnation from the Lord above. When you deal with condemnation, you are dealing with feelings of guilt. Those feelings of guilt are the trap that engulfs many of us and may lead to us being in a depressed mood. Remember, find that peace. For me, I have the bible that helps me with the peace that I need. I hope that you are able to have something that helps freely give you that foundation for peace that I so love and experience on a continual basis.

Once again, when you destroy the power of the chatter thought entity, you are now able to give birth and grow the planning thought entity and the present thought entity. When you start doing this, it is here where you have taken over your mind. You are no longer someone who is being controlled by thought, which are your chatter thoughts, but you are someone who is waking up every day with their mind being that of the planning entity, and the present entity. When you put these muscles of thought in your brain to work, it is here where you can finally start living the life that you were created to live. It is here that you can finally start planning, start creating the life that you've always wanted, and start living in the present. For when you live in the present moment, that is where you can start truly experiencing the fullness of life.

The sad thing is that there are people who have never been able to escape their chatter. For years and years their chatter thoughts have taken over their thinking. Many of these people have gone through seasons of their life where they have been depressed and have gone through moments of anxiety. When you look at someone who struggled with chatter thoughts controlling their lives, you see that this individual never truly lived. They were just individuals who lived on this earth and were constantly consumed by their chatter, taking away the peace that they so long for and craved.

The great thing to know is that you will no longer wake up and realize that for the last 30 years, when you were at work you were thinking about your family. You will never think about the fact that every time you were with your family you were thinking about what you did not do at work. You actually are living in the present because you have put to death your chatter way of thinking. To live in the present is where you need to be in order to experience life to the fullest. Now how beautiful it is to experience life to the fullest when you had planned your way to create the life that you've always wanted to create.

As you enter this new journey in life, you must realize that you will be able to take control of your life. This will be such an amazing moment in your life. Ever since I have applied this principle to my life, I have seen my life change drastically for the better. Each year I notice how more and more my life is changing. A huge reason for this is because I have let the peace rain in my life which has washed away my chatter way of thinking. What this has allowed me to do is to give more in growing my planning way of thinking and my present way of thinking.

Of course there are problems that arise. I remember when I used to have problems that would cross my table. My initial thought was to try to get rid of the problem. As soon as I started acccpting that everything happens for a reason, and that life is happening for me, I started seeing problems as gifts! Jim Rohn once said, "don't wish things were easier, wish you were better." When I notice a problem arise, I now see that there are areas in my life that I need to learn to grow in. For example, if you are someone who seems not to have enough money at the end of the week, one thing you should do is work on your spending habits, or take a financial course. What I am trying to point out is that when a problem arises, I don't get beat down, telling myself how I messed up. What I do, is I don't acknowledge the chatter thought that I have felt, accept that everything is happening for my own good, and start planning on how I can get better, while working on the present moment to get better.

How freeing is it knowing that you have accepted your uniqueness, which is the greatness inside you, and have also made the decision to go after what you always wanted to go after, while at the same time being in a position where you are in control of your mind and your thoughts!

Now, even after we have been able to capture and take control of the internal enemy, you have to be aware that there are things externally that you cannot change and have control of. The family you were born into is something you never get to pick.

Your father, your mother, and your siblings are those external forces that we must also see how they were placed in our life for our advancement of our true purpose in life. What lessons are they here to teach us?

So many times, we think that our family members hindered us from accomplishing what we were meant to accomplish in this world. When in all reality, you will be surprised to learn how much your family plays into the fulfillment of your path. Oh yes, your family is a key in unlocking your true purpose in life! Now let's look at our family to see what a true blessing they are and have always been. When you acknowledge this, it will fully wake you up to further prepare you in helping you fulfill your true purpose for your life. Here we go!

5

The Family Gene

Some of us have family members who we owe the world to. There is no way we could have accomplished everything we accomplished if it wasn't for them. For me, one of the biggest factors that helped me accomplish everything I've been able to accomplish is my parents.

My dad instilled in me to be a man of my word, and to never take shortcuts in life. I remember growing up as a kid how he would have me picking up all the papers outside in the front yard. I must have been like 10 or 12 years old at that time. The last thing I wanted to do was be out in the heat. So, what I would do is I would rush the process and only focus on the big papers that were outside. At first it looked like I had picked up all the papers. I then would tell my dad that I was finished. He would take me and show me where I had missed some of the papers. I mean some of the papers that he would notice were smaller than my thumb. I thought, "Are you serious? How is it possible for me to pick up all the small papers?" The thing was, I was missing the point. The big lesson here was that my dad did not want me to take shortcuts. He wanted me to take my time looking at every area of grass as carefully as I could. I will never forget a time later where I tried to rush it again.

Man, did my dad really let me have it. Even though that might seem like a very insignificant moment, it really did impact my life. To this day I notice I have a very difficult time cleaning the car as quickly as possible. If after cleaning the car, and putting everything away, I still notice a spot on the car, I will take all the cleaning supplies and make sure that the car is clean. There are moments where I am outside cleaning and pruning a branch, and my wife will call me in. After 15 minutes of her telling me to come inside, I eventually go inside after 20 minutes of making sure that I pruned all the branches correctly.

As for my mom, she was someone who constantly vocalized that she believed in me and said that I could accomplish anything I desired to accomplish. I clearly remember when I was thinking of joining UIL, University Interscholastic League, in middle school. To be honest, I did not feel I was adequate enough, because in middle school the only kids who were going to the UIL meets were the smart kids at the school. I remember when I mentioned it to my mom and she said that she believed I could do it. I don't know if my mother knows, but I was one of the individuals in last place. Even though I was not winning, my mother still encouraged me. It made her proud that I was a part of the UIL group, but she also truly believed in me. Because of this, I eventually believed that I could start taking Pre-AP classes with those students who were in UIL in middle school. I eventually found myself in the same classes as they were. All throughout high school, I was able to make the top 10% of my graduating class. Some attribute this to my hard work and all the extra-curricular activities in which I participated. To be honest, it was because my mother always believed in me. Her belief in me is what got me to believe that I would be able to accomplish everything I set out to accomplish.

Unlike me, some of us have parents that have held us back from being the people that we wanted to be. Some of you might say that you never had a father who was there for you. My wife's story goes that at a very young age she was raised by her single mom. Soon thereafter, at the age of 5, she went to go live with her grandparents to be raised by them. She was able to live with her grandparents until she was 19 years old. Soon after that, she lived with her aunt and uncle for the next ten years, until she met me. Then, after we got married, she came to live with me.

Even though she had her grandparents, when my wife talks about her life, I can tell that there are moments she might have wished that her life would have been different. Especially when she would see that a lot of her friends growing up had both their mother and father. At first, it can seem that my wife missed out on the benefits of having both her biological parents in the picture, but in all reality, her life situation did a lot of amazing things for her.

When I hear my wife talking about the things she has a heart for, at times it correlates to the little girl that she once was, and her heart goes out to those people who might not have their mom and dads. Her biological father and mother not being involved in her life is what actually pushed her to make sure that she married someone who would be there for their child, and she would make sure that she would be there as a mother for her child.

If you have never seen the movie, 'Collateral Beauty', I highly recommend it. It shows how a lot of things on this earth that have hurt us have actually molded us into the individuals we have become.

The thing is, none of us get to choose which family we are born into. I mean who would not love to be born into a family where your family was rich and your mom and dad loved you and supported you all the way. This is a kid's dream.

Whether we had good or bad influences, in order for us to live life to the fullest and take control of our lives, we must not let our external factors get in the way by thinking that they did nothing for us. *This family gene either helped you become the person you were created to be or it helped you desire those things you did not have growing up.*

Marcus Aurelius once said, "What we do now echoes in eternity". I am a firm believer that the family we live in has its own particular purpose in order for us to be able to live the life that we live. Often because of our experiences, many things get in the way that don't let us see how valuable our family can be to us.

There are many situations where problems or conflict have arisen with a family and people are hurt because of the situations. At times the situations prevent individuals from talking to one another. I have heard many stories of brothers not talking to family members. Sons and daughters not wanting to see their parents for a particular reason. I believe that our family is a clue in order for us to figure out our true purpose in life. **It is what I like to call the family gene.** This family gene will help create your identity. When you understand your identity, it will help better prepare you to tackle the challenges on the road to success.

It is my hope that through your understanding of the power of your family gene, you will forgive any family members that have hurt you. To hold any unforgiveness against anyone, especially a family member, can be a stumbling block that will continue to trip you up on your road to success.

Unforgiveness is a thing that I believe has trapped individuals and prevented them from truly being able to live to their true potential. When we don't forgive someone, and then we do forgive them, we realize that the prisoner all along was ourselves. This cannot be seen more clearly than when we hold grudges or bitterness against our family members. What we need to do is let go of these grudges and forgive our family members, so that we are not prisoners. Forgiveness is the only way to be able to walk through this door and into that new journey in your life so that you can be able to live the life that you're supposed to. There is no way you can accept your uniqueness, be great, make the decisions to control your mind, and accomplish your true purpose in life without accepting your family gene. Whether you see your family gene as good or bad, you must see it as a guidance to your true purpose in life. The people that you must forgive the most is family. Forgive them and forgive yourself.

So many times we think that the world owes us things. When in all reality, the world will give back to you what you give off. When it comes to family, there are times when many of us don't call our parents, or brother, and sister because we feel they should be the ones to call us. You have got to get rid of this thinking. Do not wait for your family members to show you love and affection. Since you are someone who has greatness within themselves, and has made the decision to live life to the fullest, and has now taken over the mind and thought and has a belief system that is founded on peace, you should be the one to show love to your family. Choose to love without trying to get any love back.

I can recall many times in my situation where I've had a disagreement with my family. My father and I would get into disagreements. There were many times where I felt my father was being disrespectful. I am not going to say it was easy, and it took some courage for me to do, but I knew what I had to do. I had to forgive my father in order to not be a prisoner and entrapped.

After I forgave my father, he was left with the choice of whether or not to be upset or accept my forgiveness. Each and every time, even though he was the one that started the dispute, I would still forgive him. I am very grateful that he did accept my forgiveness. I mean come on, when someone is genuinely asking forgiveness, whether they were the one who was wrong, it is difficult not to accept their request for forgiveness.

I am very glad that I took the step to forgive my father even when I had no reason to forgive him because of what he had done. Had I not done this, I would have lived with much regret when he unexpectedly passed away in 2015. Remember forgiveness is the key that will release you from the bondage that you are in. Plus, you are living life to the fullest. You are not about holding grudges anymore. You are about living in peace and wanting to share that with everyone, especially your family members you come into contact with. So, let's do it.

Let's pick up the phone right now and call our family members and forgive them!

Let's do it! If you're still holding back, you have to realize that the only way I was able to forgive my father was because I was able to take some time and think about my father as a child, and how his father never taught him how to ask for forgiveness. The stories that my father would tell me about my grandfather is that he was there, but he was never really there. I bet there were so many times where my father wished his father would have been there when he was younger. This eventually ended up transpiring later in my teenage years where I can say that my father was there, but he wasn't really there emotionally. No one ever taught my father how to really share emotions from a father to a son. This is the reason my father had a difficult time acknowledging when he was wrong. There were times when I would forgive him, that he would eventually come to me and let me know that he had realized he was wrong, he just did not know how to bring it up.

What you have to do is gain a deep understanding of why your parents and your family members are the way they are. It has a lot to do with changing your perspective, and that is what we have to do when it comes to our family. When you change your perspective, you will be able see how your heart goes out to each of your family members. Through the process, you will begin to pick up different attributes and attitudes you picked up from your family, and how they have helped create the identity you have. My hope is that when you see how much you and your family members have in common, you will grow into a deep appreciation of all your family members and in turn embrace all that makes you who you are. Like they say, we don't get to choose what family we are born into, but I will say we get to experience the pride of the family gene we were given.

Hopefully by now you have accepted that you will forgive all your family members. The freedom you will feel inside is one that you have so been longing for. What I want to do now is go through my father, mother, and my siblings. You will notice that there will be times where I do not hold any unforgiveness, but through a deeper perspective, I get to see the family gene that we all have and how we are all connected.

When I think about my mom, I see a very strong woman. Taking the time to understand your family members will allow you to carry the pride you need to make it on your journey of success. My mom is a woman who at a very young age had to learn to start working hard. I recall stories from my grandma, that even though my mom was the only girl among 5 boys initially at the time, she was still one of the hardest workers. I mean imagine having to be raised in a household of all boys. I bet there would be several times where you would have to prove to everyone that you were capable of fending for yourself. Growing up, I never knew why mom was such a strong lady. To be honest, I think I have only seen my mom shed tears once or twice in my lifetime. No matter what people thought of her, my mom was never going to let her current situation dictate the outcome of her life.

So, just by looking at the life of my dad and my mom I see that my dad was a person who never learned how to show his affection as a father to a son. This explains why growing up I longed for that affection from other sources. I constantly found myself trying to get along with other male role models and seek their approval. This helped create an inferiority complex. I would constantly be trying to seek the approval of everyone that I would come into contact with. It was as if I was trying to hear them say, "I am proud of you". This eventually led to me letting go of seeking the approval from anyone when I learned that there is a God who is proud of me and loves me.

Rarely hearing that my dad was proud of me led to me accepting how much I was approved and loved by God above. My father not really telling me that he was proud of me led me to truly accept how much God was proud of me. The downside of my earthly father created the upside of my heavenly father. The gene that I take from my father is that his emotional absence created a huge opening for my heavenly father to show me that I am approved and loved by him.

The gene that I carry from my father is that of love. Because of my earthly father's lack of affection, it led to me receiving the love and affection from my heavenly father.

Knowing that this family gene came through my father, it is clear that the family gene that also came from my father was that of forgiveness. Because of this, there have been several moments in my life where I found myself loving the things that no one seemed to love, or easily forgiving people. One of the messages I recall from the speech that my best man gave at my wedding was how he had never met someone who was so forgiving. This right here is a blessing that I will forever and always be grateful for from my dad. If it weren't for him, I would not have these forgiving traits.

I think about the life of my mom. I think about her experiences and how she always had to show that she was good enough. There are many challenges that she had to deal with her life. Then, I think about my grandpa and how he had to work years and years in order for him to be able to provide for my mom and my uncles and aunt. Had my grandfather not done that, my mom, including myself probably would not be living in America today. This family gene that I take from my mom is that of the power and blessings that will come from hard work. No wonder my mom always believed in me. She truly believed that with hard work anything is possible.

As hard work became a part of my life, I reflect on how in order for me to have reached where I am in life, I had to work hard. It is at this very moment that I think that the only way that I made it through my years at Michigan State University was through hard work. But there are many different definitions of hard work. Hard work can be that of working physical labor. Hard work can be that of reading a ton of books. Although in essence, hard work is the persistence and determination to fight through the resistance of anything that is in front of you that might try to stop you from reaching your goal.

I can honestly say that I am proud of the person I am today. I am proud to say that my grandfather was a migrant worker, and worked hard so that my mom and her siblings could live in America. I am glad to say that my family's experience of not having much is a part of who I am and this has made me the person that I am today. It is through this acceptance of my family that I gained a special love and appreciation and I end up embodying these family genes. It is a feeling deep down inside that burns for them. Deep down inside I truly love my brother, my sisters, all of my uncles, my cousins, my parents, and my grandma.

Before any of this, my family was a group of people who I just called my family. I can say with much pride that my mom is the strongest woman I know. My sister Graze, is one of the hardest working women. My brother Josh, who has shown unlimited potential overcoming challenges. My little sister, Vanessa, makes me proud every time I think of her and she's one of the smartest people I know. These are all individuals I truly care about and love. And my dad, who is in heaven right now, I am very grateful that the last couple years before he died, he is someone who I truly saw as my best friend. Though we had disagreements, I truly loved my dad for the many things I was able to learn through him.

Some of you will say my life was completely opposite. I had a father who wasn't there. I had a mother who abandoned me when I was young. Or, I have a brother who has been a rascal to me my entire life. What you need to do is to realize the collateral beauty behind all those experiences. If it wasn't for your father leaving, it would not encourage you one day to be a father who is there for his kids. If it wasn't for your mother leaving, it would not have instilled in you to find a woman who would love her children. As for your brother, it is probably so you'll be able to understand what some of your kids will go through, and will prevent your kids from being rascals to their own siblings.

One of the most amazing things about my family that I have come to realize is that they make us into the individuals that we are today. We are there to get the good traits they've installed upon us. Or, we pick up the traits that we so long for, and did not get from them. Therefore, we have to take a step back and be very grateful and thankful for these people that God brought into our lives, for it is because of them that we have been shaped into the person that we are today. These are traits that we picked up along the way and will be genes that we will pass on to our kids.

For me, one of the biggest lessons I ever got from my family was learning the value of education. Being that no one in my family ever got a four-year degree, it pushed me to get an education. Another attribute that I was able to get from my family was the value of hard work. It was instilled in me since I was a kid, learning what my grandpa and my parents had to do in order for us to have the life we have today. Another thing that I got from my family was always believing that I could accomplish whatever I wanted to accomplish. I remember as a young kid, my mother telling me that I could be whoever I wanted to be as long as I put my mind to it.

It is important for you to take some time and find pride in the family that God allowed you to be born into. No matter how dysfunctional your childhood might have been, you have to change your perspective and see the good or at the very least, see the lessons as a gift. When you see the good, that is where your appreciation for your family will come. It is this pride and appreciation that will allow you to walk on the road to success with greater joy and fulfillment.

It is one thing to walk through life and become very successful, but it is even sweeter to know that along the way you have so much appreciation and pride for your family. I truly believe that by doing this you will be able to inspire others around you to do the same. As you help them liberate themselves from the lies that their families are not important to them, part of you going on the road to success is the journey. Taking your family in your heart on the way will definitely make the journey sweeter.

Now think about it. One of my goals in this book is that you get to a point where you are living life to the fullest. When I say living life to the fullest, I mean seriously *LIVING LIFE TO THE FULLEST!*

Sure, it's one thing to have your friends join you at the table of success, but to have your family members there is even more amazing! The characteristics and traits we pick up from our family will help determine how much joy and enjoyment we will get on the journey we take in life. Along this journey, we will meet people who will become our friends. We will also be drawn to certain career paths along the way. What we have to realize is that it is not the friendships we build along the way, or the career paths we take, but it's the things we learn about ourselves from our friendships and careers that will help grow us and guide us on the journey of life that will lead us to our purpose.

6

Friends

Now that you have reached a point in this book where you see that your uniqueness contributes to your greatness, you must make a decision to go after what you have always wanted. Once you do this, you have also reached a point where you have defeated your mind and your thoughts through the peace of your belief system. While at the same time, you were growing the appreciation and pride of where you came from. You are now someone who is truly living life to the fullest. Now you can start discovering what you were made for.

Once a person starts unraveling what they were made for, it is one of the most amazing feelings. What hurts me is knowing that there are some people who never get to experience this. Helping people figure out what they were made for is something that I am truly passionate about and truly desire for everyone to figure out. The desire to figure out who you are and your life's purpose is something that is truly integrated in each and every one of our lives. There is no way around it. One thing we must realize is how on the journey of life we will definitely meet people along the way.

You have to understand that there are 2 external forces that we cannot control, but we can change our perspective to have these external forces work on our behalf. If we aren't careful these outside forces can hinder the road we take for the journey of life that we are on. You are already complete inside. The only thing you need is to know that we can't control these external forces, but we can make them work to our advantage, and that's what we have to do. We will make sure that we will choose to see the cup half full, instead of half empty. One of the external forces that you will naturally come into contact with is people. To dive even deeper, the first external force will be the friendships we create. To go even deeper, this will also be the significant other the good Lord brings into our life.

The friendship with these individuals will either hurt us, or help us learn things about ourselves that we would not be able to learn otherwise. Our different experiences with friendships will also begin to shape us, and can even help guide us to where we are wanting to go in life. It is obvious that the people we hang out with are the people we end up becoming. My grandfather had a better way of saying it. If you hang out with crap, that is what you start to become. But, if you hang out with success, that is what you end up becoming.

Alexander Nehamas said it best, *"We become who we are in great part because of the friends we have."* We end up hanging out with many of the people that we do because we were raised with them or we met them at a school. The world we live in leads us to interact with many different people which also leads us to create numerous friendships. But what is the purpose of our friendships? Is the purpose of our friendships so that we can talk to them and just hangout with those people? Or is there something that draws us to those people to learn more and discover more about ourselves?

Growing up I had a friend that I would hang out with quite a bit. Later on in life, he and I ended up becoming best friends. We both were also one of the best men in each of our weddings. On our first two encounters in middle school, we actually got into a fight. Little did we know that a couple years later he and I would end up being best friends in high school. But when I really think about what drew us closer together, after reflecting on it for a while, it was clear that it was our love for competing and our desire to win that brought us together. Many times we found ourselves competing with one another. This led to us hanging out more than usual.

Many other friendships are brought together in a similar way. Whether it's your love for sports, or being raised with similar beliefs and values, or that both are artistic people, there is a reason we become friends with the people that are actually our friends.

In high school I was involved in cross country. I will never forget my freshman year, when my coach suggested that I compete in the varsity team. Even though I had never competed on a varsity team, I said yes. It was no surprise that I came close to last place. I had gotten smoked. But even though I was beat, something inside me elevated me to keep working hard and competing in those cross country meets. It wasn't until my junior year in high school that I finally started placing in the varsity meets.

By this time, my desire was not to place on the varsity meets, but was to make it to State. Man, I wanted it so bad. I mean no one had ever gone to State in my family in any sport. To be honest, no one in my family was ever a runner before. It's not like I had the genetics to make it to State. What pushed my desire to want to go to State was my love for competing. I loved competing. I can honestly say that my true experience in competition did not really take off until the taste of competition I got from competing with my friend from middle school. It probably had a lot to do with me making it to State for cross country and being the 32nd fastest 5K runner in the state of Texas in all 3A districts at the time. That was also the reason I was able to get offers to go run in New Mexico. Crazy to think how much my love for competition paved a portion of the way to my success.

Some of you might be thinking, "yeah, but the friends that I hang out with are not real friends. They constantly bring me down. And they're always discouraging me to not do what I want to do". If you are in a friendship like that, my advice to you is to cut those friendships immediately, and to find the friendships that are actually worth your time. You need friendship in your life that will make you a better person. So many times we are in toxic relationships and we wished we had different friends. Well you can start doing that today.

"Yeah, but what are they going to think about me?"
"What are they going to say?"

Okay, let's seriously get rid of that chatter thought right now. Remember, you cannot control the future or the past. Now what I want you to do is take out a sheet of paper and write a list of the names of people who help you out in life. As for the ones who do not help you out in life, you know exactly what you must do. To be honest, cutting out the friendships in your life is not difficult at all. Remember, why would you want to seek the validation of someone who keeps bringing you down, and who does not have a lot going for them? These are the last people that you want to be your friends out of everyone in the world.

Do you not know how many people are in this world? You have got to take a deep breath and see. There are not millions of people, but billions of people on this earth. Let me give you a better perspective here.

Say for example there was a new born baby. Let's say that from the first day that baby is born until it reaches 120 years old, this baby gets introduced to a new person every minute. Every minute they would get introduced to one new person for the next 120 years, 12 months out of the year, 52 weeks, 7 days a week, 24 hours a day, and 60 people every minute. The interesting thing, that even after 120 years of this individual being introduced to 1 person every moment from the day they were born, they would "have only met less than 1 percent of the entire world population. Now look at that. This fact here is so true in giving you the perspective that in this world you will only ever be able to personally ever meet less than 1% of the entire world population. So why not make those people that will be a part of your life, people who are there to uplift you? If you wanted to, you could literally cut all your friends out of your life right now, and make new friends! Just like that! Keep in mind, I am saying getting rid of the toxic friendships, not the uplifting ones.

Now trust me, at first it might be weird, because you have been prone to hang out with the same people. Your hanging out with them happens naturally without you even saying yes sometimes. That right there is the issue. You keep saying yes to these toxic people, or you say nothing at all. Remember you are the person in charge of your life. No one else is.

One of the best things you can learn to say is NO. Let me affirm you right now and say it again. When someone calls you to hang out you can say NO, and you also don't have to give an explanation. The best thing you can always say is that you are too busy learning from a seminar, or an online class that you are taking.

At first it will feel weird, as you are letting a lot of people down. But you have to remember that you are not letting them down, you are actually doing yourself a favor. By allowing them in your life, you are continually letting yourself down.

You have to remember that you are no longer seeking validation from other people, you already have all the validation you need. You are unique and were made for greatness. There is no need for someone to come into the picture to make your greatness complete. You are already great, and it does not depend on your friendships or the people you know. Now of course knowing the right people can help you get there, but even if they help you get there, they have nothing to do with you delivering you. You are the only person who can deliver you.

One of the biggest healers in getting rid of friends and the people that you do not want in your life anymore is TIME. I will say it again. TIME is the healer and teacher. When you decide to cut those friendships out, remember you are doing this to detox yourself from all the negativity that these people bring. Let us have this conversation right now.

Will it feel lonely at times? Yes it will.

Will you feel like you are on this journey all by yourself? Of course it will.

But you have got to realize that this is part of the process. Some of you may not know where to start, or what changes you have to make. This is a very practical change you can make. You can get rid of the people that should not be in your life and you can embrace the moments of silence and solitude. I can assure you that it is the moments of silence and solitude where I have grown so much! At first your body will have a difficult time adjusting to it. I will give you some great things to incorporate in your life that will help you with the process, but you have to be willing to go through it. When you enter these moments, it will give you time to start hearing that small voice inside you that has been drowned out by all the toxic people, all of your chatter thoughts, and all of the negativity in the world.

It might even bring you back to your childhood imagination and all the things you thought of doing when you were younger. YOU will finally make some time and plan to go on a trip you have always wanted to go on.

For me, being an extroverted person, this was very difficult for me to embrace. There would be times where I could barely even take a couple minutes and mediate or be alone. I always wanted to do something. I can tell you that I have gone from that to being able to spend some quiet time with the Lord above for over an hour, or even just a day where I am in stillness and silence. I love having a wife who understands me, gives me my space, and lets me embrace those moments in my life where I need some quiet time. For me it is during these quiet times that I seek the Lord to show me what I need to get out of my life, what I am missing, and what I need in my life.

So, will it be difficult for you to distance yourself from the people you have always been around? I will say it again. Yes, it will. But remember this is part of the process. This is what you must go through in order to figure out your greatness, or for you to grow and see what friendships you actually need in your life.

In the world today we have so many choices of friends we can make, that we barely get to see that we are the ones that choose our friendships. But you will say, I never chose my friendships, they chose me. I will tell you that is incorrect. It might have seemed like your friends found you and you chose them, but, we are the ones who attract the relationships and friendships we choose to build along the way.

When I first went to college, I had initially met some guys that were great guys. These guys were the type of people who would be willing to be there for you when you needed a helping hand. After a while I noticed how there would be new people who would eventually join the group. Many times, I would say nothing, and I would just go with the flow. That is the problem right here. Even when you don't say yes or no to the people that enter your life, you are still saying yes. I wish there was more information on building friendships and how to choose the right friends. There are many books on marriage relationships, and how to be a great coworker, but very few on the study of friendship that I have seen.

So yes, if you are not intentional in deciding who you allow to be your friend, you are still saying yes to those people that enter the relationships, and just bring their toxic lives, and eventually infiltrate your life.

You see, because of the social media we have nowadays, it has made it so easy for us to find friends, but it has also led to you being victim of becoming friends with someone who you didn't want to befriend, because you never spoke up.

As much college life went on, I then met another individual who became my best friend in college. At first this person was not like the friends I had made when I first went to college. The thing is he still liked to have a good time, just like my other friends, but there was something different about him. Unlike my other friends, whose primary focus was going out and partying, this new guy that I met, still went to college to learn and have a good time, but his priorities were different.

That's one thing you have to remember when it comes to choosing a friend.
We have to learn to choose friends who have similar priorities as we do or better,
who have the priorities that we want in our life.

The best approach when choosing a friend is to be intentional with choosing your friends. It might even lead up to you being up front with some of your friends by letting them know that you are no longer going to want to do the things that they are doing.

When I started hanging out with my new friends in college, I noticed how my old friends would invite me to places to go hangout with them later that night. To be honest, I kind of wanted to hang out with the new crowd of friends who were going to watch the Michigan state football game, grab some food, and then go hang out with some girls and guys to go bowling or go play some pool. I mean this was exciting for me. You see, before I was always someone who would try to blend with what everyone was doing, so that I could be liked. All of this changed when I accepted the Lord Jesus Christ into my heart. Now I am not trying to bring this up to convert you or even convince you. I am just sharing a solid experience that I went through.

Before I always thought that I had to earn my way to heaven, after 3 months of being in college, I learned that there was nothing I had to do to earn God's love or anyone's love anymore. The only thing that mattered was that there is a God who loves me because he sent his son Jesus Christ to come die on the cross for my sins. His doing that paid for my sins, and now it allows me to have a relationship with God that would take off in the years to come. Here I was, someone who always thought that I had to earn God's love when in reality it was freely given to me. There is nothing you have to do to earn Gods' love. It doesn't even matter if we love God or do anything. His love for us is not based on our love for him. He shows this by sending his only son to die on the cross for our sins. He first loved us. We are truly loved by God.

When I figured this out, I reached a point where I did not feel I had to stay in the relationships that I was in. Even though I had received all the peace that I needed, I still needed to be the one to make a choice and decide if the friendships I previously had were to be the friendships that I would keep.

So how was I going to do that?

I clearly remember having the conversation with my friend. I had run into him in the lunch cafeteria and we sat down and ate together. Towards the end of our meal, I recall him asking me, "So what's up man, you going with us this weekend?" It was right then and there that I finally spoke up. I said, "You know what man, I have nothing against you all. As a matter of fact, I really do like you guys. You guys are great, but I think what I am going to be doing is hanging out with some of the guys and girls I had just met in the meantime. Like I said, it's nothing against you all." After I told him this, I could see how he was just there pondering what I had just said and looking at me. After a while, he acknowledged what I said, and replied, ``That's cool man.'' Since that time, I ran into him several times and he would gladly come up to me and say, "What's up man, how are you doing?" Now this, right here, is what I need for you to realize.

If someone is really a friend, and they know that you are trying to better your life, and they see how you hanging out with different people is going to better you for your greater good, that right there is a true friend. **Those who support our growth and expansion as a person are those we want around us. That is a true friend.**

The last thing you need to have is someone who is putting you down because you are not hanging out with them. Learn to watch for these clues. Remember no one has a say in regard to the friends that you choose to make. That is your decision and no one else!

As you can clearly see, for me I had to be very intentional about choosing my friendships in college. There could have been thousands of other people I could have made friends with. I chose to make and keep my friends intentionally based on my values and what I cared about that was important to me. When those things aligned, that was someone I would choose as a friend.

When I reflect back at the friendships I made in college, I notice how many of these people that I befriended had the same priorities as I. We all came from different backgrounds. One of the perks of going to a university is all of the diverse people you will meet along the way. I was very fortunate to make close friends with guys and girls who were of different ethnic groups.

At first, I always assumed that if someone was able to go to a big university, just like the one that I was very fortunate to attend, they came from a family who had money, and who was there to support them. Man was I wrong! I came to find out that even some of the college students who came from affluent families still had to work for what they had. I noticed one thing that connected me with one of my friends was knowing that even after what he had at home, he was striving for more in life. This led to me trying to break glass ceilings. Breaking glass ceilings is something that you are able to do when you see what other people are able to accomplish. Now, here I was getting inspired, not just to go to school to become a doctor at the time, but also to be a doctor that owns many clinics and has doctors working for him.

It's like if my friends were not going to college to be in their careers and start working, but they wanted to run the companies that their dads or parents were working in. So many times, we think we can only do so much until we find out that other people are doing more than what we want to accomplish.

I was very grateful and blessed to make the friendships that I did in college. Now I will say that even though it looked like all my friendships in college were there to encourage me, there were those friendships that did not look like they ended good for me. It wasn't until years later that I could see how much of a blessing meeting that person along my journey was for me. And now, I see how not having that person in my life is an even bigger blessing. I cherish the lessons and take those with me. I leave the rest behind.

When I was in college, I also met a great girl. I ended up dating this girl because of her love for God. There were so many good things about her. Right before I graduated college, I ended up proposing to her. I felt deep down inside that I was also called to go back home to Texas and teach those kids to believe in themselves. Little did I know that my real wife was going to be the reason I would be going back home in the first place.

After nearly a year of being engaged to my college girlfriend, we ended up postponing the wedding, which eventually led to us breaking up and going our separate ways. The main reason for the break up was that she wanted to be in Michigan with her family, and I wanted to go back home to live in Texas. After breaking off our engagement, two weeks before we were going to get married, I will say, I was devastated, as anyone would be. What I did not know is that the friendship that I built with her, and what I learned through it all, was going to be one of the biggest blessings in my life.

After breaking off the engagement, I clearly remember realizing exactly what I wanted in the woman who would become my wife. This time I knew that the next person I would date would be someone who would have all the qualities that I wanted in a future wife. Now how do you suppose I knew exactly what I wanted in my future wife?

When I broke off my engagement, I knew that there were other reasons why the engagement was called off, and I was certain that the next person I chose to be my wife would be the one. Instead of this break up leading me to a world of a negative down turn, it actually gave me hope in finding that right one. If it wasn't for my ex, I would not have known exactly what I wanted in a wife.

This showed itself to be true when years later, I got set up to go on date by a coworker of mine who also had a sister who was also a teacher, and her sister had a friend. When the 2 sisters got together, they said we would be great together, so my coworker gave me the girl's number. As soon as I saw this girl, I was like "Oh my goodness, she is gorgeous!" As most guys are visual, and no, I am not lying when I say my wife looks like a supermodel.

Now the things that I want to share with you here is that even after I saw the way my wife looked, I knew that I wanted to get to know this girl before I would show interest. After hearing her say all the qualities that I wanted in a woman, that I told no one about, after our first date, I called one of my college friends and I said, "Man I am just going to tell you right now man. This girl right here is going to be the one I am going to marry." Never would I have thought that after the first date I would feel inclined to ever say that. Now I will say it took me six months for me to convince her that I was the guy she should at least consider dating. I must have asked her out to be my girlfriend like 3 times, before she told me yes. She wouldn't even let me hold her hand until she was willing to be my girlfriend. Fast forward now, we have been married for more than 4 years and each year has been amazing.

What I want you to realize that even though my ex-girlfriend was a really good girlfriend to have, my wife is amazing! I would have never realized how amazing my wife was, if it wasn't for my past relationship. Through my past relationship, I realized what I surely did want in a woman and I did not settle one bit. I made sure of it!

I truly believe that friendships are there to confirm more about the person that we are. It took me a while to realize that the one thing that brought my friend and I closer together was our love for competition and our desire to win. I have now come to realize that this is one of my strengths. Each of us has a friend that we can relate to but, if there is nothing that the person and you have in common, and you are still hanging out with them, then I would suggest you to really ask yourself why are you spending your time with this person? And be really honest with yourself. Are you bored and they always seem to have free time? Is their budget similar to yours so choosing a new place or activity seems easy because your price point is the same range? You know some of the same people and hang at the same places (it's comfy, like old shoes) or you haven't made time to put yourself out there to meet others.

As for my friendships, the friendship I built with my best friend in high school was the love for maintaining a healthy lifestyle. I remember asking him one day what he enjoyed about working out. This definitely was one of those days where I just needed some motivation, because I did not want to be there that day. When I asked him, I did not expect the answer he gave me. My best friend in high school had a brother who was the same age as my brother. Well, when his brother was in middle school his family found out that his younger brother had a tumor in the brain. Eventually his brother was unable to beat the illness, and passed away. During this time my friend was able to see how lucky he was in that he was able to exercise, unlike his younger brother, who could not go outside and play basketball. While he on the other hand could choose to get up and go any day he wanted to. He went on to say that he was able to see how there are people who do not have a healthy heart, lungs, bones, and muscles like his brother who passed away did. Because of that realization, he has made it a goal to make sure he is always exercising and being active. This is his way of showing how grateful he is to have the health that he does. This really did help shape my belief in working out. Never again would I take my health for granted.

The other thing that my friends were able to do was help me strive to excel in academics. When I was in high school, I would hang out with a group of kids that were in the top of the class. Seeing what they were shooting for, what colleges they were wanting to attend, ended up pushing me, and is what helped me want to go to a university outside the state of Texas.

Lastly, friendships also helped me to realize the type of woman I would marry. There were certain things that I liked in certain individuals, and other things that I did not like. One of those things was a woman who was to herself. Keep in mind, it's true when they say opposites attract. I am someone who can be very talkative, unlike my wife who is very quiet. But I like this about her because she has what I do not have.

I strongly believe relationships are there for a reason. They are there to help you realize some of your strengths and your weaknesses. When you have nothing to compare to then it is really difficult to really understand what you are about. It is vital that you re-evaluate your friendships. The person you hangout with does not have to be exactly like you. What you do need is to see how these friendships are helping you realize your strengths and weaknesses. Through your friendship it is important that you also grow as a person.

Growing as a person is vital in determining who you are, where you are, and what you are wanting to do, in order to live the life that you have always wanted to live.

Throughout my years I have been very blessed with the people that took their time to invest in me and pour knowledge in me. One of those individuals was a man I met in college who became like a spiritual father for me. He was that pillar I needed when I did not have my family there. I had never witnessed a man who truly showed humility in the way he lived his life. His embodiment of humility was something that I admired and made it a goal that I would incorporate this into my life. Now keep this in mind that I can be a very prideful man, especially when I try to think about everything that I have accomplished on my own and don't acknowledge that it was the good Lord that deserves all of the credit.

Another reason why it is vital to choose your friendships carefully is that they will help you regarding your health. There is so much research out there that talks about how having good friendships can help decrease any cardiovascular disease or other alignments. When you have a healthy friend, they can also be helpful in keeping you accountable that you are staying up with your exercise goals. And, it's not only with your exercise goals, but also with other areas of your life where you may need support.

Now that you have chosen to get on this journey you need to understand part of this journey is that of personal growth. The personal growth topic was not something that I knew much about until after I graduated high school. It took a lot of work on my own to read these books, listen to several different podcasts, and attend several seminars. I was surprised to see how not a lot of people who I had previously hung out with knew much about personal growth, or any well-known personal growth speakers. What you have to realize is that these personal growth communities exist out there. You just have to be intentional in finding these groups. Many times, we don't realize it, but the people we have been hanging out with have a fixed mindset, and have settled to have a fixed mindset.

The difference between a fixed mindset and a growth mindset is that someone with a fixed mindset does not think they are able to change the trajectory of their life. They believe that some people are born to be great while other people are not born to be great. Their minds are fixed, in that you cannot change where you are going in life. The growth mindset is very different. A person with a growth mindset knows they can actually change their life, and be who they want to be. It doesn't matter who your parents are, what family you're born into, or what genes you carry. What does matter is that you are willing to put the time and energy to learn what you need to do to be successful. You are willing to put in the time. Even if it takes you 20 years to become a lawyer, that is okay. The thing that matters is that you became an attorney. It doesn't matter how long it took you for you to get there.

You can easily tell the difference between a person with a growth mindset and someone who has a fixed mindset. Typically, it has to do with goals that people have set for themselves.

So, one of the key ingredients in finding the right friendships is surrounding yourself with people who have a growth mindset. These will be people with goals. My advice to you is the next time you start talking to your friends, start asking them what goals they have in their life. If they brush it off, and change the subject, that should be a warning to you that they probably have a fixed mindset. But if you ask your friends what goals they have and they start talking about what they want to do, and the goals they want to accomplish. This right here should let you know that they have that growth mindset. So even if they don't know about personal growth as a concept, they have the potential to enter a season of personal growth. They just don't have the guidance.

Now that we see how this external force, friendship, can really have an impact on our life, we have to pay attention to the next external force that we all deal with. The next external force is the different seasons that we all go through. Not only the external force of our family, our friendships, but the new seasons we encounter. We all are in a particular season, some of us are entering a season of sadness and hurt, while others are about to enter a season of happiness and abundance. What we must do is realize that the external forces of the season that you are in is what is guiding our seasons for our highest good.

7

Different Seasons

As we travel our life's journey, along the way you will encounter the next external force that you have no control over. This external force is what I like to refer to the different seasons we experience in our life. Many times we go through a season where it feels like there is no way we are going to make it. What you have to realize is that life happens. Let me say it again,

LIFE HAPPENS!

At first it may seem like there is nothing we can do about this, which is true at first, but that can easily change. In life we experience many seasons.

The seasons of life that I would like you to focus on are as follows:

1. The season of joy and happiness

2. The season of heartache, pain and upsets

3. The season of working

4. The season of learning and growth

WE are all in this life together. We all go through the same things. The only difference is that each of us are in different seasons. As my good friend Eric Thomas likes to say, "you are either going into a storm, either in a storm, or either getting out of a storm".

There is also a scripture in the bible that I feel lays it out beautifully for us: In comes from the book of Ecclesiastes:

There is a time for everything, and a season for every activity under the heavens: a time to be born and a time to die, a time to plant and a time to uproot, a time to kill and a time to heal, a time to tear down and a time to build, a time to weep and a time to laugh, a time to mourn and a time to dance, a time to scatter stones and a time to gather them, a time to embrace and a time to refrain from embracing, a time to search and a time to give up, a time to keep and a time to throw away, a time to tear and a time to mend, a time to be silent and a time to speak, a time to love and a time to hate, a time for war and a time for peace. What do workers gain from their toil? I have seen the burden God has laid on the human race. He has made everything beautiful in its time. He has also set eternity in the human heart; yet no one can fathom what God has done from beginning to end. I know that there is nothing better for people than to be happy and to do good while they live. That each of them may eat and drink, and find satisfaction in all their toil—this is the gift of God.

When I was in college there were several times where I did not know where I would get the money necessary for me to make it. Man, those five years in college that I spent out there all by myself were very difficult. I clearly remember the moments where I would be in college and would be in the dorm all by myself on Thanksgiving week because I did not have any money to go home. I will say that during this time, there were moments I felt like just going back home. It felt as though there was no one there who would understand me. Another moment in my life where I was in a season of storm was when I also stayed in the dorms during Spring Break for an entire week. No one was in the dorms. I was all by myself. The only thing that I would do was go to work and then head back home from work. There were also those summers where all I did was work. I clearly recall in college having to work 3 jobs at the same time, while making sure I was still a student.

Now I will say that I had a great time at Michigan State. The friendships that I gained during that time were priceless and forever shaped my life. But, as for the season, it was completely opposite. Even when I was going to school my first year, I found out my parents split up, on top of the fact that my grandfather had passed away. My grandfather was a man who I had grown very close to over the years. There were times at night when my grandfather and I would just sit outside and talk. He and I would have these amazing conversations that I will forever treasure.

During my time at college, I also found that it was very difficult for me to adjust to the culture shock that I had experienced. I soon found how a lot of my peers seemed to be more advanced than I was. It was not that they were smarter than I. It was just clear that they had been able to have more life experiences than I had. Growing up, I clearly remember only taking a couple of trips. I never really left the state of Texas. As for my college friends, a lot of them had traveled to several states around the country. Some of them had even gone abroad. I truly feel one of the best things a person can do for another person is give them the opportunity to travel to an area they have never visited. This will definitely open their eyes more to the knowledge that is out there.

In all, you can see that season that I was in was a storm. It was definitely a season of struggle. But what you have to realize is that even though there were many days where it looked like I had no reason to get a degree, it actually became one of the best experiences for me.

When I found out that my parents had separated, I was devastated inside. I clearly remember talking to one of my relatives and them letting me know that they thought I should really consider coming back home. This was definitely something that I truly considered, as it hurt me that my siblings were going through what they were going through being there in the middle of it without me. Even though all of this happened, I can honestly say that it was the biggest blessing in my life. During this time, I had already dedicated my life to the Lord and had made the decision to not blame either of my parents for what had happened. In turn, what I did was allow myself to see that in the end everything would work out to our advantage. It did not matter what season I was in, but I was certain that I would eventually go out of the season. I knew that during this time it would make me stronger. I knew that as much as I wanted to go home to help my family financially, I knew that me finishing college would be the best thing for me to do. I knew that the reward would be greater in that I would eventually get a degree and have enough money to help my family. During this time, I just had to make sure to persevere, and trust that everything would work out for my own highest good. During this time, I did have a choice to make. I could choose to be upset, and hurt, and a victim. But instead, I chose the opposite. I chose to have faith that eventually things would work for our good.

At first it looked like it would not, but I can honestly tell you that years later, things did work out for the better. Eventually, I was able to graduate from Michigan State and three months later I found myself working as a full-time teacher, making more money than I had ever made. It definitely would have been easy for me to be a victim during this time. And, it is easy to let this happen. But what you have to do is you have to change your perspective regarding the season that you are in. You have to look for freshness, like with each of the annual seasons. Seek out the lessons and blessings that you are being gifted. Every season has a reason.

During these times, you will discover a different side of you that you never really knew you had. You will begin to take form and become someone stronger, and better.

In this life, we will go through several different seasons. What I need for you to do is gain a different perspective in the season that you are in so that you can see that things are working for your benefit. Just because you are experiencing a season where it might not seem that things are working out for your good, you need to trust that it is.

Once again, you have to remember that you have no control in life except how you respond to what happens. How would I have learned that my grandfather was going to pass away when I was in college? It was my hope that he would eventually be able to say that he had a grandson who made all his work of coming from Mexico to the USA all worth it. I never got to experience that, and just the thought of it right now hurts my heart. But what you have to realize is what that did for me. Knowing that my grandfather was unable to celebrate me graduating from a university and earning my bachelor's degree allowed me to experience the bitter sweetness of success. It got me to see that even though you make it to the top one day, it doesn't matter, if the people you hoped would be there, are not there to cheer you on. Man did this really open my eyes. I was under the impression that when I became successful, I would be able to have everyone there with joy and happiness cheering me on. Well, I am here to tell you that it did not happen to me. I was very fortunate to graduate from Michigan State, but I did not have my grandpa there to congratulate me or see my success. Also, my parents were split up and my siblings were struggling financially. Is this what happens when life throws its problems on your parade? There has got to be more to this I thought, and there is.

A couple years later I found myself working as a teacher. Not only was I a teacher, but I was on my way to getting my master's degree. I was working full time, coaching, and in the evenings, I was taking the classes. I remember the time I told my dad I was working to get my master's degree. My goal was to be an administrator, and then to become a superintendent at the time. I remember how proud my dad was of me. Man, how amazing it would be when I earned my master's and then for my father to see that his son received his master's degree, become a principal, and then a superintendent? All was going well until the day of February 22, 2015 came.

I was just about to call it a night when I was in my room ironing my clothes. Then all of a sudden, I get a call from one of my dad's coworkers letting me know that my dad had been in an accident where he rolled over. I kept asking him if he was okay, and he kept avoiding the question. Eventually I asked him to tell me if my dad was alive or not, because either way I was going to find out. Then that's when I heard the heavy words that came from his mouth and said, 'no your dad did not make it, he passed away'. Later that night, I felt like I couldn't breathe. I remember also spending all that night crying. It was at that very moment when my life was going to change forever.

You know I had always heard of these moments, and similar experiences that people go through, but I had never experienced this much pain before in my life. I mean I had experienced the passing of my grandfather, but the pain I felt from the passing of my father is something that I wish on no one. The next thing I knew, I had to let all of my siblings know. Each and every one of them would rely on my dad whether it was moral support or financially. To go through the pain is one thing, but to have to deliver the message is another thing. I remember that right before all this happened, I was very excited with my career. I would even talk about how I was going to work to eventually change the education system in our nation.

Well after my father passed away, all of this came to a stop. I can honestly tell you that I did not think of my teaching job, my master's degree, or much of what I was trying to do to succeed and make things happen in this life for myself and my family. I seriously recall literally being numb for the next two weeks. What I want you to see is that when life throws the season of heartache, pain and upset your way, things you think you cannot bear, you have a choice. One choice is that you can let this season destroy you. Or, you can use this season to make you stronger.

Surprisingly after all the hurt, the one thing that I kept thinking about were a few words that my dad had shared with me. My dad had shared with me several things during the time he was here on earth, but for some reason the one thing I kept hearing from my dad was, "Son, life is too short, you have to make the best of life. Tomorrow is never promised" The words "tomorrow is never promised" kept coming to my head.

Soon after my dad passed away, I started reflecting on my career, about life, and asking myself what I really wanted to do in life. I knew that I enjoyed teaching, but when I asked myself if I saw myself doing the same thing I was doing, would I be satisfied? That is when I came to the realization that maybe teaching wasn't the thing that I was supposed to do. What I decided to focus on was the one thing that I would talk to my dad and my family about. I would tell my family that the one thing I would love to do is open up my own business so that I can be financially free and not have to rely on someone or something putting food on the table for me. Little did I know how much my dad passing away was the one thing that was actually going to point me to the new direction in life I would take.

When dad left this earth, it was very difficult for me knowing that I would never see my dad ever again. I would never be able to share with him my success or the business that I had wanted to start with him and my brother. The one thing that it did for me was actually point me to the thing in my life that I had so often wanted to do. Because of my dad's passing, I truly realized that life is never promised, therefore it is very important for you to go after your dreams no matter how crazy it sounds. You have to be willing to go all in. I can only imagine how my dad must have felt knowing that he never got to accomplish everything he wanted to accomplish. I remember when I was younger and my father would tell me stories about how he would eventually like to own a couple rental houses. This intrigued me. Well, I am glad to say that even after my father passed away, and the season tried to get the best of me, my dad's passing actually made me stronger. Five years after my father passed away, I can honestly say it is the best thing that has ever happened to me besides me accepting Jesus Christ into my heart, and meeting my wife.

The life we live will throw many different things at us. In the end, we all have a choice to decide what we are going to do. The choice is up to you. There is a tribal story that goes, "A wise chief said that we each have a good wolf and a bad wolf inside of us who are constantly at war trying to come out of us every day. A young Indian from the tribe asked the chief, "which of the wolves comes out?" The chief replies, "the wolf that you feed the most is that one that comes out."

The seasons of life will provoke the two wolves inside you to want to come out. It will be your choice to determine which wolf you are going to feed. After my dad's passing away, I could have so easily stayed in my teaching career, which would have been okay. Or I could have just quit teaching and not cared about anything, but I did neither of those things. The one thing that I did was feed the good wolf inside me with the decision that I would go after my goal of wanting to open up my own business.

Life throws us many seasons, but the decisions you make are determined by your perspective. Had I looked at my dad's passing, as a way of seeing that life is pointless since at any moment you can leave this earth, I would have chosen to just quit my job, and care less about anything, but I did not. The perspective that I had was that he might not have been able to do what he was unable to do, but I was ready to do what he wanted to do and more!

Now that you are living the life that you have always wanted, it is truly an amazing feeling. I personally am grateful that I can live how I am living each day that God has chosen to grant me. Every other day from here on out is a blessing. Any moment I can spend with my family is amazing, especially with the work that I do, and with my dear friends. This circle of love is something that I am very blessed to experience every second of my life. They say that to be rich and feel empty is one of the worst places to be. It is better to be a poor man, that feels rich which is the best place to be.

I am not saying that troubles will not come. Because troubles will come. Now, how you handle those troubles is a different story. You can choose to focus on your troubles as challenges that will disable you, or you can choose to say that you will learn from those challenges. One of the key aspects here is to be able to change your focus. When a mountain of a challenge comes, you can complain (which there is no need to, especially if you are already living the life that you are), or you can think of different ways to get past that mountain of challenges and have fun along the way. Constantly changing your perspective is important for you to remember when challenges come your way.

Desires and Expectations in Different Seasons

Another important thing to remember is to also understand the difference between setting expectations and having your desires. I remembered when I first learned this. I learned this in my relationship. Many times, when we expect something to happen, and it does not happen we get upset. Yet when it does happen, we accept it as if it was supposed to happen and there is nothing to it. When we decide to have desires, and something does not happen, we are okay with it. But when it does happen, we are really excited that it happened. It is very important to understand the difference between the expectations and desires that you set for yourself. This in itself can really help you in the little things that are not that necessary to deal with.

Now I am not saying that it is not important for you to have expectations. Expectations are necessary. If not, we would have people showing up to work and things would not be getting done in time. What I am telling you is that it is important for you to really evaluate whether or not the expectation that you have should truly be an expectation and whether our desires should really be desires. Understanding this will allow you to live your life simply on a daily basis.

So, be aware of who you are and how your current perspective on things affect how you see life. Some might say, "yeah, but not everything is tied to desires or expectation", or others might say, "wow, I can see how some things are tied to desires and expectations'. So, let your perspective be one that assists you in living your best life, THE INTENTIONAL LIFE!

8

All About the Journey

While reading this book, you might already be in a career that you love, or a job that you do not want to be at anymore. What you have to realize is that working at the job you are at, has its purpose, even if you don't see it. As for me I have gone from being a teacher to a full-time real estate investor. Little did I know how much my experience from my previous work would best prepare me for where I am in life right now. In the journey of life, we all have to work, but seeing how the work you are doing has its role in you fulfilling your true purpose in life, is key.

Work is something that everyone is raised with. Since the day we were born, we are raised to be taught to work. Many of us from the very beginning try to stay away from work. The reason why is because anything we decide to relate to work is something that we do not want to do. Whether it is to throw out the trash, wash the car, or clean our room, we hate it. The reason for it is because there is obviously no connection to the purposes as to why we are even working.

If my parents were to pay me for work, then I would be very motivated to work. That is because I would understand the purpose. Or if my parents said that the only way I would get the new XBox was that if I were to work for it, then I could relate. Before I knew it, that entire week or month I would be working very diligently to do the work that my parents wanted me to do. So quickly on, we noticed how when there is a motive as to why we should work, we end up wanting to do it.

Early on we are not taught to work for things that we want. We are forced to go to school. Forced to sit in a classroom and listen to the teacher talk, instead of being able to decide what we want to listen to. As a teacher, I would always see the irony in my students who wanted to learn, but when I told them what we were going to be learning about that day, the comparative adjectives vs superlative adjectives, they at times were resistant to what they were going to be learning. The thing is that deep down inside we all love learning. At times when I gave them the option to decide what they wanted to do, it was as though they were totally new students. They became students who were asking questions and who wanted to work in class. Obviously through my direction, the students were able to complete the work that was asked, but it was evident that they were more motivated to complete it because it's what they wanted to do. So, it is really interesting how it is evident that we are okay with working when it is something that we want to do. I truly believe that this burning desire in us is something that motivates us to want to work, or better yet, go after what we were created to do.

If there is something that motivates us to want to work then it is very important for us to figure out what is that purpose for us to continue working. So, what is that purpose? Why is it that we do not know our passions and work for jobs that we do not want to work for? Why is it that many of us are working in jobs that we do not like or want?

This right here is the next obstacle that we have to tackle. Many times, when you make the decision to make a change you will find yourself in a particular job that you are already working. I truly believe that each and every one of us was made to do something. It isn't until we find that passion or desire, that the saying, "those who love their job never work a day in their life" becomes so true in their life.

A reason for us never taking the time to figure out what we want to do for work is because we are so caught up with everything that is going on in our life. What ends up happening is that we choose to settle. With all the distractions going on, many of us are unable to take the chance to reflect about the things that we really were made to do for work. Instead, what we do is look at what everyone else is doing. Many times, our decisions in life as to what job we are going to work on is dependent on how much we are going to get paid. Many times, we let the income determine what job we will work. But as soon as we start working and reach our goal, it will fill us with a sense of dissatisfaction.

Before we know it, we don't know our purpose and the days of the week that we dread the most are the Mondays. But our Mondays should be the days that we appreciate the most in our lives. I will never forget the feeling when I started working as my own boss and running my business. It was as if my Mondays were something that I would look forward to. This feeling was something that I had never experienced before, but what made it very different was that after 6 months I noticed how every Monday was still the day that I was looking forward to. It's as though I had experienced something that I had never experienced. What was this change?

It is clear to say now that what made that happen was that I finally felt purpose in my life. I was no longer working at a job where I felt I had to in order to provide for myself and my family. Knowing that I was working on something that had a purpose is what motivated me to wake up every Monday eager for the day.

This right here is what you have to do. You have to make sure that you're working at a job or profession that you know you were created for, or that is at least a stepping stone to get you where you want to go. Seek to make connections with others on your same path. Use it to learn new skills that will help you get where you are going.

I truly believe that your work is not something you should feel obligated to have to go, or feel forced to go, but it should be something where you can't wait to get there. Whether it is the fact that you like sewing and animals, then your life should consist of sewing clothes for animals. But, why do we not do that? Why do we let the outside things dictate our life and determine our jobs? What we need to do is stop and reflect. But some of you might say, "I cannot leave my job. My family is dependent on me providing for them." Just you saying that is the reason why you still keep going to that job.

Imagine for a second that you did not have a family and you had all the money in the world. I know you have probably thought of that scenario before, but before you respond, I would like for you to add something else to it. Right after you think of that, I would like for you to think about the person that you are. What type of person are you? Are you someone who likes working with people, or likes working alone?

Are you someone who loves to travel? Whatever it is, start reflecting on the person that you believe you'd like to become. The thing that you'd want to be able to do if there weren't jobs in the world. What would you like to do to make the world better? Or what would you want to discover? As simple as these questions are, they are important for us in figuring out what type of work we should really be doing. I think it is so easy to write off the little things in life when really at any moment your life can change with a word of advice or a thought. The thought of you going to go to the store, or to the park can lead you to meet a long-lost friend who may become your wife, or husband. *The key to figuring out our purpose in life is taking time to reflect.*

This is key!

Reflection is the answer. Growing up, I was never taught to reflect. I was always told where to go, and what to do. Later in my college life, I started doing a lot of reflecting. You will be surprised how much you can learn and discover about yourself if you just take some time off.

When I was a teacher, I did have a desire to start a business. The next thing I knew was that my father passed away unexpectedly. During this time, I started REFLECTING on what I really wanted to do. The next thing I did was I looked to see how much money I had. I had enough money saved where I did not have to work for a year. I could actually make the decision to live off that money without working. Now this was going to be a risk, but I was going to take a risk on myself. So many times we are willing to take the risk and rely on someone else to come through. We take the risk to go to work and rely on our boss, or the company we work for is going to bring our paycheck. We take the risk of missing our kids' games and we are working so that we can go on a vacation later, when the best joy you can experience is right then and there seeing your kid playing a sport.

Why is it that when we take a risk, we leave the results on someone else's shoulders? When in reality, the only person that makes the reward come through the risk is yourself. You are the one who is working, not your boss. Your boss is just there to make sure you have clocked in every day of the week. All they do is sign your check at the end of the week. So in the end, when taking a risk and the reward that comes from it is dependent on you, why don't you take the risk on yourself? Aren't you already doing this?

Now trust me when I say that when you take a risk, and it is clear that it is dependent on you, you will survive! There is so no way around it. All of us have that nature inside of us. If we do not have a job and we had a family to feed, we would find a way to put food on the table for our family. Even if you had to start cutting grass, knowing what you had to do to make sure that your family was taken care of would all of a sudden come naturally. Now would it be hard? I will say it would just take time. So how about we start thinking and be willing to take a chance on ourselves.

I have had people tell me, "Wow! that's crazy to think that you left a teaching job". And I also left being contracted by Teach for America where I was training teachers from all across the country. Imagine if I were to tell them how I turned down a curriculum instructor job after I got my master's degree. I think I will just keep that to myself.

Well from an outside perspective, it does look like it was crazy for me to leave a secure paying job, especially after I had just gotten an offer to be a curriculum instructor and use my master's degree and make more money. The thing is that the secure job that I had was dependent on other people coming through and making sure that I was going to get paid wasn't really that secure for me. When I realized that at any moment the entire education system could change, or they could delay me getting paid. I had to ask myself, what would I do? Then, I imagined what if they were to start laying off all the teachers who only had 10 years of experience and less. I am talking hypothetically here but this really got my wheels turning. Now, what if I did not work as a teacher and I had my own business? I was the one who would be in charge. I was the person who had to make sure I was going to work to try to put food on my table. Then let's say the entire public education system collapsed. At the end, it would not matter because I had made my own way. I had bet on myself that I would be the one to bring in the capital necessary to support my family. This right here was one of the reasons why I also left my profession. I wanted to reach a point that if anything ever went wrong, I would not have to worry about it.

Now out of these two scenarios, which one do you think is most secure? Obviously me going out and wanting to start a business was riskier. But it was only riskier in the beginning. I was taking a bigger risk in life relying on another source to help me make ends meet, instead of relying on me, the true resource to provide for my family and me.

Another thing that crossed my mind when I was working as an educator was that I was working so many hours. I remember I was working Monday through Friday as a 6th grade teacher. Then as soon as I would get out of work, I would be coaching after school up to like 7pm, and I would not get home until around 8pm. Then, I would also get home and be working on preparing the assignments for the students the next day. Then on Thursday, I had the football games to coach and I would not get home until 10pm sometimes. Then on Friday, I had the varsity football games. Sometimes I would not get home until 11pm, especially after those away games. Then on Saturday, I would have to wake up early to go coach the B-team game and wouldn't get home until around 3pm. Wow, I still can't believe I did all of that. The crazy thing is that during the time that all of that was happening, I was working towards getting my master's degree. I think you figured out what days of the week I was completing those assignments.

Now, I am not going to say that doing what I was doing was wrong. There are some people that have been put on this earth to be educators and coaches. They have found their true calling in life. With some of the coaches I worked with, it was evident to me that the Friday night lights are what they were called to do. As for me, after my dad's passing away, I came to realize that everything I was doing was very exhausting. I had to take a step back and ask myself, what is the one thing I wanted to do? What was I created for?

For some, you all have probably already done things. You have these ideas in your mind that you have longed to do, and you do it. But others, we have similar desires and ideas but we do not execute on them. The reason for it is because we feel that there are a lot of things holding us back. If you are relating to me on that, my advice for you is to reflect on those things that are holding you back from truly reaching your goals. Once again, this is the key element to figuring out what you have truly been put on this earth to do. It definitely starts with you taking the time to REFLECT. Even though you might not have that figured out right now, the thoughts that do come to you are the stepping stones that will lead you where you want to go in life.

I'm here to tell you right now that if you do feel you have figured out what you were meant to do in your life, it will be amazing when you enter a new season and see how life just keeps unraveling itself for you.

When I started working as a teacher, I truly felt that was my true calling in life. I got to the point that I was ready to one day change the education system. Then all of that changed for me after my 5th year of working as a teacher. Little did I know that a new chapter was about to start. The lessons I learned as an educator only prepared me for the next steps I was going to take on my life journey.

When I was working as a teacher, I realized early on in my career that I really enjoyed learning as much as I could. This actually ended up transpiring in other areas besides the classroom. I found myself working to get my master's degree. I also found myself getting into reading a lot of personal growth books, and people's biographies. I was very fascinated to learn how someone, or anyone, could become great. What did they have to do to get there? I truly believed everyone had greatness within them. What decision did these people make that led them to be successful? I also grew in my learning about investments, and real estate. This is something that stayed with me ever since college, after I read that Rich Door, Poor Dad book by Robert Kiyosaki. I knew that eventually I did want to invest in real estate, or invest in some sort of business, and even open up my business someday. Keep in mind, this was back in college. I just did not know when, and since I never really shared it with anyone it would not matter when I started it.

I know the thing that my job was able to also do for me was help me realize that I really enjoyed inspiring my students. I remember as a teacher I eventually became coach as well. There were several times I would take some time right before the class was going to end, and I would just be speaking truth to my students, inspiring them with different words of wisdom. Even as a coach I would recall telling my football players that success on the field started in the locker room, and in the classroom before it took place on the playing field.

Another thing that I enjoy as a teacher was taking risks. I enjoyed taking a concept that we were learning and I would create scavenger hunts for my students. I remember as a teacher standing on the top of my desk with the tie over my head and explaining a concept to my students. I remember telling my principal that if he would just trust me with all the risk I was taking as a teacher he would see the results at the end of the year. I am glad to say that the results came in when our school had the highest passing scores of the entire 6A school in the district. Of all the teachers I was the teacher that had the highest scores. Now I will share with you that it did not start with having 80% plus of my students passing the state mandated exam. It started with me only having 50% of my students pass the state exam. During this time, I remember calling different teachers all across the state wondering how their kids were able to accomplish what they were able to accomplish. This helped me realize what I needed to do to get my kids to the next level.

One of the last things I learned from being a teacher is that I could not see myself working within the confined walls of the classroom. As much as I like teaching, and inspiring my students, I knew I was designed to go out into the world and make my own path. I knew I always wanted to start a business. I also knew that investments, and real estate was something that always interested me. All of this changed when I got invited to a real estate investment seminar. It was there where I asked myself, "how come I have not started a business, or better yet, how come I have not taken the leap of faith and started a real estate redevelopment business?" I knew that the reason I wanted to start a business was because I wanted to be independent and not have to rely on anyone.

I also wanted to reach a point in my life where I could be financially free, and could also one day give a home to my mom. After my father passed away, and I took time to reflect, I realized that my true vision in life was to be financially free. My purpose in life was to create capital to ensure that the right leaders were in right places in the marketplace, and so on. This was my true vision for me. It wasn't being a teacher. Yes, I had at one point been on fire for being a teacher, but I knew that there was more that I wanted to be. The only reason I was a teacher, and a coach, and had worked hard to get my education was so that I could make enough money for my family and me just to be content. After my dad's passing, I knew that I didn't just want to make enough money for me, but I wanted to also give back to other organizations and groups. I wanted to create capital to help families, business, government, schools, etc. The vision for me grew, and that is what I want to focus on right now. Your vision!

Now the question that I want to ask you is this.
What is your vision for life?

Where there is no vision, the people perish. - Proverbs 29:18
Without a vision, you will become an individual who will one day find himself walking aimlessly in this world.

Or Hellen Keller says it best. Hellen Keller was an individual who was born blind, and deaf. Even though she had many obstacles that she had to overcome, she was able to accomplish so many great things here on earth. One day they asked her if she felt bad for not having any sight. Where she then responded, "the only thing worse than being blind is having sight but no vision."

Little by little I saw my vision start to expand! It wasn't until in 2015 when I learned that my father passed away unexpectedly that it really started to unfold. One day my father was driving this truck and was rolled over and was pronounced dead immediately. I remember hearing the news. It was very devastating for me, as my father was like my best friend. But what it did for me is that it got me to ask the question that I am going to ask you right now. If you knew that tomorrow was never promised, what is the one thing you would want to do? What is the vision for your life?

For me, I knew that I really enjoyed learning, and also enjoyed taking risks. I also knew, through time and time again, that if I put my mind to something, I could accomplish it. It was right then and there that I knew I would be leaving my education career. I decided to open up my own real estate investment business. I knew it was a risk that I would take, but as my mom would always say, "Son, when you put your mind to something, you always end up accomplishing it no matter what it takes."

After spending a couple of weeks mourning my loss, I spent the entire summer REFLECTING. I even ended up leaving the school that I had been teaching for the last 5 years and went to go teach at another school. I knew change was coming and I was ready for it!

During my sixth year of teaching, I started writing my vision down on several pieces of paper. It was during my sixth year of teaching that I opened up my business. After my father passed away, the only thing that mattered for me was making sure that I would finally be able to do the things that I've always wanted to do, since tomorrow is never promised. My goal was to create a business where I would be financially stable, enough to support my family, so they could be able to spend more time together.

That's what I wanted!

You see after my dad passed away, the one thing that I kept hearing over and over was that tomorrow is never promised. I debated with the realization that this was true. What was even more devastating for me was knowing that I would never get time back. **It was time!**

You cannot put money on time. Time is given, and it can so easily be taken away. As valuable as time is, it is free, as long as you have it.

But when it's gone it's the one thing you wished you had more of. So, it was time that I would be fighting for!

I knew that if I stayed as a teacher, time would pass me by. I wanted to make sure that I did whatever I could to make sure that I could make the most of the time I had. This meant me going all in on starting the business so that one day I would not have to work and not have to go to work if I did not want to. So I made the leap of faith, and I left the teaching profession after my 6th year of teaching.

Now after starting the business, I had no idea how much time it was going to take. I was under the impression that as soon as I started the business, shortly thereafter I would start making money, but this is the exact opposite that would happen. I actually did not even make any money the first 11 months of being a business owner. During this time, I found myself working so much. There were times I was working close to 80-hour weeks. I remember taking a step back and asking myself, "How am I working all this time, but don't even feel it?"

The reason I did not feel it is because I had connected it with my vision. Every day I would wake up I would think about the vision that I wanted for my life. I remember waking up at 3:30 am in the morning and looking at my wife and my son sleeping. This would just motivate me to go after it. I was not going to lose the time that God would give me with my son.

So I went to work, before I knew it, I finally started making money. In just 3-4 months I had taken home more money than I would make in one year as a teacher. This was astounding to me. Wow, it was actually working. What I did not realize is what was actually taking place during all this, and this is what I want you to take out of this chapter.

All of us have a purpose in life. When you figure out that purpose it can be one of the most exciting things for you. The only thing that ends up happening is that we get so focused on wanting to accomplish our vision that we take for granted all the other things that matter.

Even though I was finally making that money to create the financial freedom for my family and me to have more time, I eventually noticed how I had taken time away from my marriage. 'Til this day I know God has given me the best wife in the entire world. For those of you that are waiting for the right women, believe and trust that God does have a special woman for you. He did for me and she actually had all the 40 plus qualities that I had wanted in a wife.

Now the story of how God led me to my wife, and her journey is a book for another day. Biggest thing to keep in mind is that God has created you and knows the exact spouse you need to make it in this world. You might not realize it, but your significant other might actually be the biggest blessing for you if you just change your perspective.

Now back to where I was, I had neglected time with my wife. Here I was growing the business and noticed how it was also taking time away from my son. I was caught off guard, and then I did some REFLECTING.

When you finally take the leap of faith to accomplish what you decide to accomplish, it is very important for you to have a vision. The vision you have for life is to remind you where you are going.

The reason we all have a vision is so that we can all know what journey we have to take in life. It is the journey in life that matters, not the destination. Now that's why I wrote this book.

So many times we don't realize what is in front of us now. We all want to better ourselves. Many times, when we decide to go after something we have always wanted, we end up forgetting about the things that really matter.

Why do you work? Or why do you have the vision for your life that you want? For some it might be because they wanted to take their kids to Disney World. They work for about 5- 10 years to take their kids to Disney World. During the time that they are saving money, their kids are grown up. They feel that if they can just make that trip it will really bring happiness and joy for their kids. So, it's that happiness and joy. That is why we all want to be successful. That is the reason why we all want to pursue our true purpose in life. It's so that we can experience the joy and the happiness at the end of the journey. But what you have to realize is that you already have joy and happiness right now.

A little while ago, I went into the kitchen to eat. After eating, my young son called me into his room. At first, I knew I had to go finish this chapter I was working on, but decided to go along with him. As I entered his room, I could see the joy he was experiencing. After a couple minutes of him being there telling me about his shapes and counting his dinosaur stickers, he picks up the football. I could tell he wanted me to play catch with him. I then started throwing the football back and forth with him, and at that moment I started feeling such joy. Especially when I saw him catch the football that I had thrown to him and how much joy he had. I could not believe that I almost walked away from this priceless gift I was feeling. I am so glad I chose to play a little bit of catch with him. Eventually my wife came in and started to record us.

The joy that my son was feeling was the same feeling he would feel when I take him to Disney World. My wife also started taking pictures. I could sense the joy in my wife when she saw the joy in my son, and all the fun that I was having. Even though we were not at Disney World, the feeling of joy in the moment that we were all filled with is equivalent to the feeling that we would have if we would have taken a picture with Mickey Mouse. To be honest, this joy was probably better in that it did not cost us anything out of our pockets to experience. We all have access to this, we just got to pay attention.

We are constantly fed the lie that the only way we will be able to experience pure joy and happiness is with all the different accessories that are in the world. Like a new car, traveling to Paris, snowboarding, going to New York, buying you the latest iPhone. In all reality, these are just the accessories in life that will assist in bringing that joy and happiness. The point of us having a vision in life is not so that we can get to our destination.

The point of your vision and your true purpose in life is that you can experience and enjoy the journey along the way.

We have it all wrong.

Along the way you will meet many amazing people. You will have moments where you cry, you will have moments where you get hurt, and even those moments where you laugh uncontrollably that you start crying. It is the moments in our journey that matter.

Our uniqueness and greatness weren't so much to get us to see the destination of where we were going, but it was supposed to allow us to see the journey we were supposed to take and the blessings on that journey we experience. **This is life right here!**

The main purpose in this life is to take advantage of the time and embrace the things and people we encounter along the way. It is one thing to be living this life experiencing those things and never really understanding your uniqueness or being able to control your mind. But it is another thing to be awake and to go through life's journey experiencing those moments to the fullest extent. That is when you get your first photographer contract, you shed tears of joy, because you are doing what you are wanting to do, and at the same time experiencing life. That is true fulfillment.

True fulfillment in life is being able to be on the journey of life going after what you were created for, and being set free from anything and everyone around you, including your mind. This is a point of euphoria that you cannot buy anywhere and it is available at your disposal if you take everything I have said in this book and I apply it in your life.

When I finally came to the realization that life was not so much about the journey, but it was about the moments you will experience on the journey, I started reflecting on the things that really mattered in this life.

Since then, I have come to realize that there are 10 things that a person deals with throughout life. Making sure you are giving attention to each of the things in your life is what will allow you to take your life to the next level and go beyond just living a life of true fulfillment and enjoying the journey of life. You will be able to have all those things including having a balanced lifestyle. No longer will you be someone who is going after their goal in life, but you will be someone who is going after their purpose in life, and also have an amazing marriage, and a great healthy lifestyle.

This is the goal of the book. This is one of the main reasons I wrote this book. It was for you to realize what you were created for. Once you realize what you were created for, you see that it's the journey that matters. Now don't let anything pass you by. You never know when you might see your son do something amazing that you take a picture of and years later you look at that same photo very grateful you were able to experience and capture that moment in life.

What you will notice is that along the way, certain things will start happening that you did not expect. You will begin to get that contract that you always wanted. You will meet the love of your life, and you will even go on the journey and meet the friend you never had before. Part of me wanting you to get to this point is actually to allow the amazing experiences on this earth to flow to you.

Now my book should have finished here, but it would not do justice if after doing all this you notice how you have done everything I have told you to do, but your health is something that has not changed. What I will do now is share with you the 10 things that I work on, on a daily basis, in order to put my life in a state of TRUE EUPHORIA in every area of my life! After I share with you the 10 things that will allow you to have a balanced lifestyle, I will then share with you the HOLY GRAIL of what is able to make sure that everything is glued together. I mean let's be real, most of us don't wake up saying we love working out. For those who do, it probably took a while to adjust. It did for me, but since then I have embraced it. Most agree that budgeting their money does not come easily to them. If that were the case, then why is there even such a word as budget your money? Alright let's dive in!

9

The Balanced Lifestyle

I remember when I first took the steps to start the business. I was working seven days a week, waking up at 3 AM, and sometimes only sleeping for about two or three hours a day. Before I knew it, I started asking myself if I had really made the right decision of leaving the education profession to focus on a real estate investment business. But what I did not realize is that I did not have the right tools in place in order for me to have a successful business.

What I realized was that I was spending a lot of time working in the business, but was spending very little time focusing on my marriage. I'm so grateful that I have a very loving and understanding wife and that she has had patience with me during this entire process. I also noticed that my friendships were also beginning to lack, as I was spending a lot of time on the business trying to pursue my vision in life, I was neglecting the other things that were important in my life. Many times, when we decide to run after our life's true purpose, we are so focused that we forget to give time and attention to the other things in life that matter. For me, it was the business and the desire to be financially free that was taking my time away from my wife, my kids, and even the friendships that I had.

We need to realize that when we are spending so much time trying to go after what we were created to do, it is because deep down inside we feel we are not really going to make it. We therefore give an aroma in the air that we do not have the things we so long for or are trying to accomplish or get in this world. Therefore, it takes longer for us to accomplish what we are trying to accomplish. In order for you to get what you want in this world, you must remember that there are several components, and that you must be balanced in your life so that you can have things flow to you and work for your own benefit instead of you trying to do it all on your own.

There's no joy in building a multi-million dollar business, if your marriage isn't doing well. There also is no joy if you have to go to the doctor's office once a month in order for you to make sure that your sugar levels are where they are supposed to be. In order for you to really create a success path to your true purpose in life, you must have a balanced lifestyle with the things that matter in life. When we have a balanced lifestyle, the flow of your business, the outcome of the career that you were building, the vision you are trying to attain will begin to happen in your life. You will notice that you will start accomplishing things you weren't able to accomplish before.

Throughout my life I've come to realize that there are 10 things that matter in my life. What good is it if I am successful in the business, but I am not making time for my family, or my kids. What good is it if I have such a great and healthy lifestyle, but my finances are out of control, and I am accumulating so much debt? What you have to do is to make sure that you are giving enough time and attention to these ten things in your life that matter. When you give attention to these things in your life, you'll begin to flourish in the business that you are trying to create or your life's true purpose.

It sure took me a while to realize what were the main things that matter. I have now been able to narrow it down to the 10 things that I must keep an eye on. You must be intentional with these things so that you can maintain a balanced lifestyle. The 10 things to maintain a balanced lifestyle are as follows:

1. Your spiritual walk

2. Your loved ones

3. Your health

4. Your personal growth (your learning)

5. Your finances

6. Your relationships/friendships

7. Your Job/Career

8. Your Thoughts

9. Your Legacy

10. Your Routines

In order for you to excel in what you're trying to accomplish in this life you must have a balanced lifestyle. In order to create a balanced lifestyle, you must make sure that you are keeping track of each and every one of these areas of your life. Doing this will bring you true fulfillment and create the euphoria that will allow you to know that you are living life to the fullest.

The first thing that you must do is take some time to reflect and then rate yourself to see how you are doing in each and every one of these areas. What you do is you rank yourself on a scale from 1- through 10 on each and every one of those items. So, for example, if you know that you have not been spending much time with your wife, or your kids, you would probably give yourself a score of 3. If you are someone who has their finances in check, and is out of debt, but does not seem to have his spiritual walk in-line, then you would give yourself a 9 for your finances, but like a 3 for your spiritual walk.

When you go through each and every one of these important things in your life, to live life to the fullest would be to get a score of 100 at the very end. I have come to realize that I may not ever get a score of 100, but as long as I am striving to work towards a 10, that is what matters. This is what is giving me a balanced lifestyle. When you create a balanced lifestyle, that is when you start to notice things start working for you. The only way to experience this is to put yourself in my shoes and try it out for yourself.

Now in order to make sure you are excelling toward a 10, it is very important for you to set goals for yourself in each and every one of these items. Now this will take some time, but it will be very rewarding for you. Man, will you look at that you are actually thinking of making goals! "But how do I set goals," you might say? Well, this is where I am going to take some time on each and every one of those items and talk about how we can create practical goals. Hopefully by my sharing the goals that I created, it will help you create your own goals. I will provide several examples for you to use. Now, I will be able to help you with the different examples, but the thing I will not be able to do is commit to those goals for you. You have to commit to it. Whether the year has already started, or it's the end of the year, in the end it doesn't matter. What matters is that you are willing to make those goals. Let's do it. Let's start off with the one goal that some of us might never even have thought about.

1. *Your Spiritual Walk*

Most of us are on our own spiritual journey. Some people have found God at a very young age, when their parents took them to church. For others, it took a lot longer as we never had anyone to guide us to go to church, or even explain to us anything about God or a greater power. Whatever journey you are in your spiritual walk, you must remember that there is always room for growth. If you are someone who claims to believe in God, but you barely go to church, or even pray, or spend time with God, or maybe help out your church, you may need to re-evaluate these beliefs. You will begin to see how you score regarding your spiritual walk—it is like a 1. Now I am not trying to say that you have to do all these things to make sure you are in good standing with God. What I am saying is that the very first thing you must do when it comes to making a goal is that you must reflect and see where you are and evaluate how you are doing.

Some of you might not know how you are doing. My advice for you is to go and ask someone who has the same faith as you. But not just someone that has the same faith as you. Someone that you look up to. Someone that you know has their spiritual walk in-check. You see we all have an understanding of what is really good, and what is not. If you have no point of reference, go to someone that you know who does, and talk to them about it. The great thing here is that they will give you a whole new perspective.

I remember when I first started growing in my faith with God. I noticed how a lot of my peers who had already had a relationship with God would say that they were looking forward to their devotion time. Some would even say that they were looking forward to their quiet time. At first I thought, "What is a devo time, or what is a quiet time?" Eventually I was able to figure out that it related to them going alone on a walk and talking to God, with no distractions. Well, that made sense why they called it a quiet time. I also learned that they called it a devo time because that was the time during the day where they were going to devote that time for God. I was very intrigued by this. Eventually I started asking questions, like what do you do in your quiet and devo time, and that's when they shared with me that some people listen to worship music, while others actually journal to God, or even read the bible. Some even choose this time to meditate to connect with and be with God.

Eventually after hearing this I started incorporating in my spiritual walk, and now had something practical to do. Another thing that I noticed was that a lot of my friends, who had been walking with the Lord longer, started sharing with me that they had a goal that they wanted to go on a mission trip this upcoming year. In other words, they wanted to give their summer up so that they could go share the word of God with people who did not know the word of God. I was like, "Wow, this is very interesting". As I kept growing in my walk with the Lord, I was able to pick up new things for me to do so that I could grow in my spiritual walk.

Some of those things consisted of sharing my faith with people, reading through the entire bible in two years, to only reading 4 chapters of the bible a day, to committing to doing a fast, to serving in the church for a season in my life, to helping the homeless, or even just making sure that I was doing a morning or night prayer. Either way, what I was able to pick up from people were the several different ways I could grow in my walk with God.

So, where are you? What are some goals you can set for yourself? Remember you are not competing with anyone. This is only for you to make sure that you are growing in your spiritual walk. Each and every year it will change depending on what new habits you have been able to establish.

The biggest thing to keep in mind when you are setting any goals is that you have a time when you are going to stop and reflect to see how you're doing. So, setting up a time will be very helpful, as it might lead you to eventually change your goals through the years.

2. *Your Loved Ones*

This is actually one that I look forward to. I never knew that you could actually make goals in regards to your loved ones. I was just under the impression that you could make goals with things like your career or your health. Making goals with your loved ones is something very important to have, as they will be the individuals who you will be spending the most time with. The thing to remember that your loved one is not only your spouse, but also entails making time for your parents, your siblings, and the one that gets overlooked a lot of times is your kids.

Many times, at the end of the year we are unsure how we are doing as parents. The reason for this is because we never take the time to make parenting goals. When you make the parenting goals you are able to see if you were able to hit these goals at the end of the year and then you are able to see how you did and where you can make adjustments and improve.

One thing to keep in mind when you are making goals regarding your loved ones is to be willing to have them input their own things that they would like. When I was setting goals for my life in this element of growth, I was thinking about how I could spend more time with my wife. When I asked her, she let me know that she really enjoyed watching movies and shows. So, what I did was to make sure that I was at least watching a show with her 3-5 times a week, and a movie at least once a week. I was like man that's good. I guess that means I don't have to take her out every weekend. I am joking. I love taking out my wife. What I was trying to say was that it's just not about taking your wife out. One of the biggest things to keep in mind is the quality time you spend with your family is what matters.

Remember it's not about the quantity of time, but the quality of time.

One book that I highly recommend everyone should read is the book 'The Five Love Languages, by Gary Chapman. This book goes on to explain how we all have a particular love language. Sometimes we think that the way we show our significant others love is through gifts. When it is not the gifts that matter, but it is the acts of service that you do for your significant other. Another book that I would recommend every married couple to read is the book "What women want, and What men want" by Shaunti Feldhahn. This is another great book in helping couples better communicate with each other. Believe it or not, reading a book on helping you with communication would also be a good goal for this element in your life. Even though that would lean more to the personal growth element, this can be a way of your knocking out two birds with one stone.

So many times, when we get married it is so easy to forget about our parents, grandparents, and even our siblings. Many times, we become disconnected from them because we never took the time to set a goal and be intentional with them. Even though your brother lives in another state, one great practical goal that you can do is to make sure you call him once a month to see how he is doing. Or one method that I have found that works great is at least planning a trip where everyone in your family can be together. It does not matter what you do, what matters is that you are being intentional about not leaving those loved ones out of the picture. Remember they are a part of you, and it will always be great to have them sitting at the table of success with you when you have accomplished some of your goals on the journey of life.

3. *Your Health*

Okay, so some things come pretty easy, and some things don't. Many times, this element of life always seems to be one that none of us enjoy. The main reason why this is one of the least favorite for people is because we set goals for ourselves that are based on other people's goals instead of ourselves.

What you have to remember here is that it is not about comparing yourself to the way others look. What you have to do is ask yourself what it is that you want. Yes, we can always go to others to give us examples as to what we want in life, but we should not say that my goal is to look like Arnold Schwarzenegger at the end of the year, especially if I am someone who has never lifted weights before. It's important to be realistic with yourself. Another thing that we must do here is that we have to realize that maintaining a healthy life is just not about exercising. It is also about the foods that we intake.

One way I have been able to change this for me is through my motto

Fitness is a lifestyle, not a hobby.

Many times, we give so much attention to other things except the foods that we eat. There is a lot of research out there that shows that much of our health issues stem from the things we put in our body. What you have to realize is that the way to change the outside of your body is by changing the inside of your body. Is this going to be hard? Most definitely it is.

I personally have been working out pretty consistently for the last 15 years. I will say that the number one thing that has really helped me stay active is having an accountability partner. A workout buddy. My advice to you, if you don't have a workout buddy right now, is to get one. Try to get someone who you know will encourage you to go after your fitness goals even when you don't want to.

Now one thing to keep in mind is that not everybody is the same. There are some people who can eat and eat and they never seem to gain weight. Or, there are those people who can work out and hit the gym and gain muscle right away, but for some people it does not matter how long they hit the gym, they never seem to gain muscle. The thing to keep in mind here is that your eating habits and your workout regimen will be very different than everyone else's.

Another thing that I encourage everyone to do is to start off small. Like if you plan to lose weight this year, set your goal by taking baby steps. If you plan to see the results and want those results to be there in the long run, my advice to you is to not take any shortcuts getting there. In the end, this will be more rewarding for you, as you will see that your results will be there for the long haul and not just for a season.

Now the last thing is the one thing that I think people leave out when they make their health goals. It is so easy to say that your goal is to lose 50lbs, or even hit the gym 4-5 days a week. The one thing that I notice people never do for themselves is reward themselves. You have got to remember to reward yourself. Many times with our health, we are constantly beating ourselves up, and there is no joy in that whatsoever. What you need to do is make sure you are rewarding yourself when you meet your goals.

So if you notice that you were able to lose 2 pounds that week, go to the nearest Academy store and buy yourself a nice workout shirt. If you were able to make your workouts each day this week, make sure you reward yourself with a nice protein shake that you don't have to make yourself, but that is already made for you. By rewarding yourself, you will see how you will be more inclined to go after your goal, than just having the thought that your health and fitness goal only deals with you punishing your body. I am all up for pushing your body to the very limit, but along the way you have got to make sure you are meeting those moments of success with rewards.

4. *Your personal growth.*

Notice that the thing you are doing here is preparing. Preparing is a key factor in order for you to be able to accomplish the goals for the different elements that you are trying to accomplish in order to have that balanced lifestyle. As for your personal growth, it is vital that you are growing not just spiritually, but also within your soul. The way you grow your soul is by being able to read different books, travel the world, see different places. As Henry Ford once said, "the more you learn, the younger you get". The way we grow younger and have a better life is by continuous learning.

When it comes to personal growth, I never knew much about this element of life until I got into college. When I decided to open up my business, that is when my love for personal growth took off! I kind of wish that I would have known a lot more about the personal growth element of my life when I was much younger. Personal growth deals with your taking the time to learn about different things you didn't know before, to better your life. There are several ways you can do this. For example, there are many personal growth conferences you can go to. There are also many personal growth books that you can read. At first you won't notice how much your soul longs to learn new things. My advice to you is to be open to new ideas. When you become open to the idea of being willing to learn, you will notice something that you never knew you had. This can be anything from learning about a different culture, to learning how to be a better communicator, to even learning how to make money. What matters is that you choose to learn about something that piqued your interest.

The one thing that you have to realize is that your mind loves learning. When you start learning a little bit about new things in your life, you will notice something inside you start to rise, that you never knew you had. You'll start noticing a hunger and the desire for more learning. This will then lead to different areas that you would like to learn.

Your mind is like a plant and the books that you read are like water. The more water the plant gets, the more the plant grows, but what is very fascinating to see is what will happen next. You will start seeing something change. All of a sudden it won't be you having to force a plan to read, you will actually willingly make some time to read. The plant will actually be the one that will be desiring the water more and more every day. My advice to you, and to those who have never been exposed to the personal growth element of their life, is to pick up any personal growth book that is out there. You don't have to try to finish that entire book in one day. You can set goals of reading one or two pages a day, or even a chapter a week. What you'll start noticing is the one thing that I noticed, and I have noticed with the people who ended up liking personal growth in their life, is that little by little your love for personal growth will change.

I remember the way I got my younger brother to start loving personal growth. Early in the mornings, my brother would be with me in my classroom before we started the day. The thing that I would tell him to do was just to read about 5 pages a day. I clearly remember when I started challenging him to read 10 pages a day and then 15 pages a day. You could see that there would be some days that he would just want to stop, but then all of a sudden it happened one day! He actually finished reading his first book. He felt so accomplished. But to go even further, he felt like he was ready for the next book. This time, I let him choose and the rest is history. This was about 5 years ago. Fast forward to now, when I asked my brother how many books he had read last year, he told me he read over 40 books. Wow, can you believe that! It was evident that the plant, which was his brain, when given a little bit of water was the one that started desiring that water. The amazing thing about this is that there is an unlimited amount of water.

Now some of the practical steps you can take with personal growth, if you have never been intrigued to want to learn, is to make a goal that you will finish 1-3 books in a year. You can even make it a goal to listen to podcasts. Then what you do is break down the number of pages that you will be reading each week. The key factor here is for you to be consistent with it. When you first start taking the steps to personal growth, there will be a pull in you not wanting to be reading that book. What you have to do is be consistent. Now if you are not someone who likes reading there are many great podcasts, and even great audiobooks you can start listening to. I encourage you right now to stop, go on the internet and look up the top personal growth coaches right now, and see which books they wrote. You will come across guys, like Tony Robbins, Eric Thomas, Les Brown, and the list will go on. Either way, you have to be practical about setting aside a time to read and learn.

5. *Your Finances*

As for your finances, some of you might have a goal that you are trying to increase the amount of money you're making every year. The most impactful goal that you want to have with your finances is being debt free. One of the practical ways you can start being debt free is by making sure that you are not living above your means. Trust me, it is not bad to buy yourself some of that Starbucks, the biggest thing that you have to do is budget for it. Once you start budgeting for it, you will be able to focus on knocking down that debt.

Some of the best ways you can start tackling your debt is by having a list of all your debts. Then what you do is focus on paying off the small debts first, while at the same time paying the minimum monthly payments on all your debt. When you finish paying the smaller debt, you will now have that paid off monthly payment to pay off the next bigger debt. Little by little you begin to start knocking down your debt, one bill at a time. While you're also knocking down the debt, it is also wise for you to start saving money. A good rule of thumb is for you to have at least 3-6 months of your monthly expenses saved. This is good. The only thing is that many people create savings, but they don't create an emergency fund. An emergency fund is an account you create in case emergencies arise. What happens is that when an emergency arises, we end up using the money from our savings account. Which is not what your savings account was intended for. The key here is to differentiate between both of these accounts.

So now that you see the importance of tackling your debt, having a savings account, and also an emergency account, don't forget to have a Spree Spending budget for you, your wife, and your kids. So many times, we don't like to hear about budgeting because it will feel like we are being limited. The only thing that you have to make sure is that you create a category within your spending. I remember when I first started this years ago. I would make sure I at least had $100 available, that I could use to buy anything I wanted. This gave me a different perspective around the idea of budgeting. Since I planned for that money, I felt like I was not being deprived because I was still able to go to the convenience store and buy some snacks.

The biggest thing with finances is that you have to be willing to make sure you are tackling your debt, saving money, having an emergency fund, and making sure you don't forget about you, before you can really start going after your financial goals. Many times, we will focus on just making sure you are budgeting all your expenses that we never create a goal.

How can you hit a target that you didn't establish? Many times, we say we would like to make more money, but we are not specific about it. What you need to do is you have to learn to be very specific about the amount of money that you want to make. When you throw out a number that you would want to make, you will notice how the PLANNING THOUGHT COMPONENT of your mind will just take off. Some of you will say, "yeah, but there is no way I can get a $10,000 raise as a teacher in 1 year," and I will tell you that you are probably correct.

Even though you are unable to get a $10,000 raise in one year as a teacher, I am here to tell you that it is possible to make that money. What you need to do is break down practically how much you're trying to make every month. So for example, if you have a salary coming in of $3000 every single month. But you would like to be making $4000, which is an extra $12,000 annually, then that means that every month you must make $1000 more. This means that you must be making $250 by the end of the week, which means that you must be making $50 extra each day. So, just stop and think about this for right now. Seriously, if you did not have a job as a teacher, and all the other places that you knew were not hiring, what would you do to make money?

Any thoughts?

Okay, but you're like, "I would like to sell something, but I got no money to get started".

Well with that type of thinking we are never going to get anywhere. For example, you can borrow a lawn mower and cut someone's grass to earn money. If you are not into physical labor, you can always fill out surveys online to start making money. What you have to realize, if you haven't already is that there are several ways for someone to make money, without using any of their own money.

Even now with an investment of $300 you can start producing your own shirts where you are buying each shirt for two dollars each and you start selling them for $10 each T-shirt. Then that tells you that all you have to do is make sure you sell 6 shirts a day, which is like over 30 shirts a week, which is normally 120 shirts a month. Now you get creative and you find that you will be able to create shirts for the city youth league baseball team. They want 600 shirts, and now you are already making over $5000 profit, and you haven't even finished the 1st quarter of the year yet!

You see, you can do it! The biggest thing that you have to do is have the belief that you can reach your financial goal. Once you have a belief and you put in some thought and effort, you will be surprised what you will be able to do.

When it comes to your finances, you have got to have the belief that there is plenty in the world. In actuality, the world we live in is bountiful. Right now, you have to know that there is still billions of dollars' worth of gold still buried underground. Not to mention the vast supply of diamonds and rubies that are still there. You have got to believe that we live in a world of abundance. When you believe in this, you will begin to notice how abundance will start coming your way. If you just have a belief of lack, you will only be attracting lack in your life. So, let's make the decision today to believe that there is plenty in this world for you to have what you want to have and to make as much money as you would like to make.

6. *Your Relationships/Friendships*

Relationships with people who are not are family members are very important to have. This is why you have to make sure that you have the right relationships with the right people. Sometimes we make the mistake of only hangin' out with people who are on the same level as we are. This is great, but chances are you will never be able to grow. I heard the saying that if you are the smartest person in your group you are not growing and this is so true. You need to make sure that you also create friendships with people who you aspire to be like, or individuals you look up to and want to learn from. A rule of thumb to keep in mind when it comes to looking at your friendships is the ⅓ rule of relationships. The ⅓ rule suggests that when it comes to all of our friendships, ⅓ of the people we hang out with should be those individuals that are on the same level as us. This is great to have as these people will be there to relate to what you are going through. Having people who can relate to what you are going through will be very helpful in your journey of life. The other ⅓ should be that of people who are where we want to go. This might be someone who is older than you and who can give you wisdom. I have come to learn that true wisdom is brought forth through experiences. Knowing that you have this at your disposal, with many older people who are willing to share their experiences with you is amazing.

For me, I have been very blessed to have created relationships with men who were 20 -30 years older than me and were willing to share their wisdom. Some of the advice that they gave me saved me from so many headaches that I would have had, had I not taken the time to learn from these guys. Lastly, the remaining ⅓ is those individuals that are not at your level, or where you would like to be, but they are those individuals that need help getting to where you are. This is good in that it will give you an opportunity to pour from your cup and to give back to these guys. There is something that happens when you are able to give advice and guidance to people that are looking for it. It's a healing within you that creates a peace that you are doing something for this world. You will be surprised to see how when you pour your knowledge into these guys, it will also be a moment where you are learning. I have come to realize that the true mastery of principals in life comes when you begin to teach it. Having people you can pour wisdom into can help in the completeness of certain knowledge you have gained from seasons in the past.

I used to always think that relationships were only created with people, but believe it or not, some of the best relationships that we can have are with the autobiographies we have read. Even though you never meet the person, being willing to learn from these people is key. It's like going to your public library and instead of paying a couple hundred dollars for you to have your own personal coach, you can get it for free!

If you do not have this relationship, my advice for you is to figure out a way to join a city sports team that you can enter so that you can meet people there. Or volunteer at one of your food drives, or figure out something you like to do where people hang out so that you can get to know people. That might be your having to plug into a Bible study as well. By the way, if you make it your goal that by the end of the year you are going to establish hanging out with certain individuals at least once a week or once every two weeks this is a great practical goal.

The key to remember about relationships is that you have to be intentional about them. Friendship will not just cultivate; you have to be willing to put in the time and effort. The little time you put in planning to create these friendships will pay you back an unlimited return.

7. *Your Job/Career*

A career is something that we all have. Whether it is us working at a fast-food place or we are a teacher, or we are a businessman, at the end of the day we all have a career. It is very important to see if the career we are in is where we want to be now and in the next five years. In order to do this, you have to ask yourself if you see yourself working at the same job in the next five years. If your answer is yes, then your goal may be to move to a higher position. If it is no, that is when you must reflect and figure out what exactly you have to do based on what you discover in your reflection. What makes you happy? What stirs your soul and makes your heart sing?

One of the best things you can do to help with this element in your life is to start surrounding yourself with people who are already doing what you want to do. I remember when I wanted to open up my real estate redevelopment business. One of the very first things that I did was I started attending the nearest city Real Estate Investment Club. Keep in mind, attending this place was about an hour away from where I lived, but I still went. You have got to be willing to make the sacrifice no matter the cost. By doing this, I was able to meet people that had been in the profession longer than I. What I realized was that there was not just one way of doing real estate investing, but that there were several ways. Surrounding yourself with the right people will be very helpful. It will allow you to see the perspective of people who are already in the career that you are wanting to pursue. This is very important for any high school student to do before they go to college. The profession we see in the movies, on shows or in the print of hardcover books is very different from the professions that we experience in person.

Once you know what you want to pursue, it is also very important to create a pathway on how you are going to obtain this goal. College advisors are very good at this, and can help you learn what classes you will need to take to get the degree you want to get. But even if you are not in college, my advice is to ask the people who are already in the career field that you want, and ask them what they had to do to get where they are. Now do not just seek the advice of one individual. Understand that there are several ways to be a realtor. Some paths work for others, and some paths do not work for you. Once you have done your own interviews and see the various paths to take, you will be able to know which is the best path for you. We all learn differently.

Lastly, please make sure that you do not choose your career path based on money. Remember that you have the uniqueness and greatness within you. When you go after the career you have always wanted, instead of a career that was based on the money you would make, you will notice you will truly be rich on the inside, as well on the outside. So many times, we think that the way to make money is with what is outside of us. When in all reality all the riches, and everything that you ever wanted is inside. When what is inside you will start to manifest, you will begin to attract the things you always wanted, the places you wanted to see, and the people you wanted to meet, which will be worth far more than the amount of money you were to make in the career that you chose for the money.

8. *Your Thoughts*

Earlier in the book, I spent an entire chapter explaining to you how you can practically take over your mind and your thoughts. Within that process, you will have to take some steps on your own to ensure that you are able to help assist you in this process.

Many times, when we set goals for different areas of our life, we leave our minds out of it. We just assume that everything is okay with our mind. But in reality, when you get to the point that you realize your mind is something you have not really paid much attention to, you have got to make sure you begin attending to your mind, especially knowing that we live in such a negative world.

One of the practical things you can do to cater to your mind is incorporate the reading of what I like to call, 'AFFEES' out loud. Your AFFEES is a word that I derived from the word affirmations.

I think it is very important to make a list of affirmations that you want to be true of you. If you have not heard of this, my advice right now is to get on your smartphone, and open up Google and type "list of positive affirmations." You will see so many links to the different types of affirmation you can have in your life.

The important thing when it comes to your affirmation is to make it a goal that you will read them every morning and every night before you go to bed. Make it a goal that you will try to do this for an entire year. You will notice little by little how your life will start to change. Here are a couple AFFEES that I have incorporated into my daily life.

1. I am positive

2. I am blessed

3. Everything that happens works out to my advantage

4. I am under God's protections

5. I am healthy

6. Good things come to me all the time

7. I am a blessing to others

8. I am a great father

9. Joy is in my life constantly

10. I live in peace daily

Keep in mind that when you read your AFFEES out loud you want to make sure that you are putting emotion into visualizing yourself with what you are saying.

Another thing that will help you take care of your thoughts is to be careful of what we listen to and what we watch. A lot of the war that we experience in our life has to do with the little battles we lose before that war. For example, if you keep listening to music that is talking about all the negativity, and you are selfish, and prideful you are losing that little battle for your thought and mind. If all you keep watching is movies with violence and horror, you are also losing the battle there. Then what you will notice is how often you have the chatter thoughts flowing in your mind.

I cannot emphasize this enough. Your eyes and your ears are the gateway to what will go into your mind. Be very careful with all the vomit that exists to try to keep you in fear. In doing this, you will notice how there will be less chatter thoughts roaming around in your mind and you will be able to live in the present moment a lot more.

9. *Your Legacy*

Legacy is one thing that took me a while to grasp how important it is. When we die, we all want to make sure that we will be remembered when we leave this earth. Even though I am running a real estate investment business right now, my goal one day is that I will be able to put a mark inside people that inspired them to be who God created them to be. Maybe that's the reason, I decided to finally write a book. This book has taken me a total of four years in order for me to accomplish it. It sure is not easy writing a book. But the thought of how this book might inspire people to go after what they want in life, and how they will impact the lives of others after them definitely makes it worth it.

Writing a book does not have to be the only way to create a legacy. You can easily attach yourself to a cause that is already going on in this world right now. You can help serve in that cause and know that you put your time in to make sure that all the abandoned dogs in this world have a place to call home.

Always remember that if you think there is nothing you can do for this world, never forget how important it is to make sure you raise kids, who will one day do great things on this earth. Many of us today don't realize how much of a legacy you can leave behind through making sure you raise great kids. So stop and ask yourself, what is something you can do to contribute for the betterment of this world?

The one thing to keep in mind, when it comes to your legacy goal, is you being willing to sacrifice your time for the betterment of a cause greater than yourself. To know that in your last breaths of life you were able to leave a mark on this world that will carry on, is what I know will help you overcome the fear of death.

The biggest fear of dying for people is not death itself, but it is the thoughts of regret, that we did not do what we wanted to do, or we are leaving this place not leaving anything meaningful behind. When you know you have made a difference in this world, it will help in assisting you to leave this earth knowing you did your part for humanity.

So far I have shared with you 9 elements that will help you keep a balanced lifestyle. The thing to keep in mind is that you must create goals in each of the elements. The best time to create goals would be at the beginning of the year. As the year goes on, it is also great to track your progress. Then at the end of the year, you will be able to see how you did, and you will also be ready to create new goals for yourself. The feelings you will get will be such a feeling that will be healing to your body. Part of you maintaining a balanced lifestyle is to holistically give you the healing your body needs, as you are on the journey of life to your destination. Now let's take time and break down the element that I like to refer to as the Holy Grail of all the elements for maintaining a balanced lifestyle, ROUTINES!

10

The Holy Grail

Of all the elements of having a balanced lifestyle, the holy grail of all of them is the routines. From the day we are born we are shown what we should do, and naturally gravitate to do the things we should not do. For example, many of us know that the best thing to do right now would be to go to the gym. But instead of going to the gym, we sit on the couch all day and watch tv, or worse yet we get on social media. It is said that the average person will spend over 5 years of their life just on social media. Can you believe that!? Wow, I wondered what we could have done with just taking one of those years and focusing on our goals and working towards them.

The thing you have to realize is that we are prone to do the things that will not improve our life. Like if I know meeting a certain individual to ask them about their career would help me learn more about the career, I'd typically would rather fill that time with being on video games, playing or just shooting some hoops. Knowing that you are prone to do what will not benefit you is why it is very important for you to have routines in your life. But, before I give you examples of the routines that you could have in your life, I need for you to understand the foundation necessary for you to have the routines in place in your life. When you have your routines in place, it's like you're creating a playing field for you to win. It's like there will be no way to fail, but first let's tackle the one thing that keeps us from having routines in our life.

It is you! You are the reason you don't have routines in your life. You are not willing to change. Many times, we are wanting a better life, but we don't even take the time to make sure we are dressed properly depending on where we are going. What you have to do is look at yourself in the mirror and realize that all the problems that you deal with are all because of you. In order for your problems to change you have to be the one to change yourself.

The other day, I heard a saying that this guy was going to try to help his team out by taking care of the problems outside that they were dealing with. Before you knew it, he was out there commanding the other guys to do this, and do that. When in reality what he should have done was taken care of himself. When he makes himself better, that's when his team is better.

Remember the best thing you can do for everyone you know is not to make sure they're okay. The best thing to do is to make sure you are okay. When you make sure you are okay, that is when you become a better person for the world. It is here where you have truly made the world a better place.

Many times, we also want other people to fix our problems, instead of us realizing that we can fix our own problems. You will be surprised to learn how much you will start changing your life once you make the agreement to work on yourself daily.

Now this is not going to come easy. What you have to realize that you will be asking yourself to do things that your body does not want to do. So, the key here is this--when you know to do something that will help you accomplish your goals, do it. Also always be willing to stretch yourself. When you stretch yourself, you will notice how making the decision to do something you don't want to do will come a lot naturally. I will never forget when I made the decision that I would take a cold shower every single morning for an entire year! (The interesting thing is that I never got under the weather during that season of my life). Yes, it was something I did not want to do. I hated every minute of it. But what I would notice is that all of a sudden, I found myself willing to do the things that I did not want to do before. I found myself making sure that all my shoes were organized in the closet. I found myself making sure to take out the trash before my wife asked me to take out the trash. I also found myself doing the things that people would say no to. All of a sudden, I saw my life start to change for the better. Once I finally started incorporating things in my life that I did not want to do, then that's when I was able to establish routines in my life and follow through with them.

One of the things that you have to incorporate in your life in order to accomplish things in your life is routines. But before you do that, you have to train your mind to do the things that you do not want to do. You have to be someone who is willing to embrace having to wake up in the morning at 3am some days. Now I am not going to say for you to enjoy it, but for you to embrace it. The one thing that I have noticed is how painful the first 3 minutes of getting up can be. If you can fight those three minutes, you will be surprised how much you will be able to accomplish that day. Wow, who would have thought that the struggle to wake up early is only those first 3 minutes. Now I am not saying just getting up and doing nothing. I am saying make it a routine that when you get up you do about 10 squats, 10 pushups, and even consider running outside in your backyard. That will for sure wake you up.

You see once you train yourself to embrace the pain, that is when you can start establishing routines in your life that will help you on your roadmap to success.

One of the first things I have incorporated in my life is having a morning routine. One of the first things I do when I get up is to thank the Lord for giving me everything he has given me. I thanked the Lord for giving me my health for another day. I also thank the Lord for blessing me with provisions in life. This is all done with a morning mantra that I have created.

The next thing that I do after making statements of positivity is, I meditate. Some people refer to it as priming. The thing to remember here is I spend the next 10 to 20 minutes putting my mind in a state of joy, and happiness. This consists of about 15 minutes of me being grateful for the heart that God has given me. Being grateful for the things that I have seen accomplished in my life. It is my way of asking the good Lord to heal me of anything I am going through and at the same time, thanking him for healing me of those things that I have already gone through. The next thing I do is I visualize myself accomplishing what I have already accomplished. When you visualize, you want to make sure you put emotion into it. I encourage everyone to start off with 1-3 minutes, and then when you get there increase it to increments of 2-3 minutes. Remember the key thing here is discipline. Now you know why I emphasize you're doing the things you don't want to do.

The next thing that I do is I read about 100 through 200 daily affirmations. These consist of those being that I am blessed, that I am loved, that I am a great father, that I have great health. Like I mentioned before, you can get anything on Google that has to deal with positive affirmations that you can read to yourself. I encourage you to make them personal so that you can be reading these on a daily basis, and as you are reading them, visualizing yourself and bringing the emotion that is attached to what you are saying. Once I finish with reading my affirmations the next thing that I do is I spend about an hour either worshiping the Lord, or reading the word of God, or just sitting in silence. This creates the balanced lifestyle of my spiritual walk.

After doing this, the next thing that I do is I spend an hour a day reading any new books that I have scheduled for the year for me to read. It is said that with one hour of learning or one hour of meditation it's like an eight-hour workday. Many times, we don't realize the value of learning. We think that the more we work, the more money we will make. Well, what I would like for you to know is that there are only 168 hours a week. At the end of the week, you can only work on 168, and nothing more. In order for you to earn more in this world what you have to do is you have to grow, and be more valuable. The more valuable you become the more the universe has to reward you for what you are worth. When I learned that my net worth would be determined by the amount of information that I knew, and not the hours I worked, my perspective on personal growth changed immediately.

Once I am finished here, the next thing that I do is I spend the next 30 minutes planning my day by going over what I am going to be doing that day. I make sure that I am making time with each of those 10 things that pertain to me having a balanced lifestyle. After about 30 minutes to 1 hour of planning, I start my day. What I do the first four hours is try to get rid of any distractions that might get in the way of accomplishing what I'm trying to accomplish. I then spend the next 4 hours going through everything I have to do. During my lunch, I listen to different podcasts, read different books, or read through my emails. I definitely try to avoid reading emails throughout the day. The biggest thing is that I try to make the most use of my time. After lunch, what I do is I spend some more time not working in the business, but on the business. You will be surprised to learn that you can definitely take your business to the next level when you pull yourself out of the business, and you spend some time working on the business. This thought alone should give you the return of investment for what you paid for this book.

Once I finish working, what I do is I go home and I put work aside, and I give my wife my undivided attention while she is making food. During this time, I also spent some time with my son. I will spend the next hour with him outside, while Mom is inside cooking food, or after we finished eating. I try to do this once a day to make sure I am spending that quality time with my son. The next thing I do is have dinner with my wife and my son, and enjoy the time we spend together. After we finish eating dinner, the next thing that I do is I make sure that my wife and I will watch a show together. This is what I call the wife time. This is allowing me to spend quality time with my wife. Once I am done with this, I then make time for myself. This could be me being online watching YouTube videos, watching Podcasts, or just being on Facebook and seeing what is going on with my friends, or anything going on in the world. Some of this time is also spent on working on the legacy that I am wanting to leave behind.

I eventually spend the next 30 minutes trying to plan my day for tomorrow, while during this time I read my affirmations.

Now I would love to say that I have done this every single day since I first started learning about the routine, but that is incorrect. The biggest thing that you have to take from me is to know that you have to be consistent. Even if you go one day not going along with the routine, you are going to have to be consistent with establishing and working on your routines.

Part of you having a routine is not to master it, but it is to try to remain consistent with it. When you notice that you are not sticking to your routine, that is fine. Just remember to try to go at it the next day.

What you will notice when you establish a routine, it will put you on a playing field to have a balanced lifestyle. After you have realized your greatness, and are going after what you want by having complete control of your mind, and you're enjoying the journey along the way, you will begin to notice things start working out for you naturally. All of a sudden you will start getting the contract you have always wanted. Life will seem to be working for you, and not against you.

That is what you have to realize that this thing we call life is always working for us, and not against us. We are the ones who try to get in the way and make life happen. But you will say, "AJ, you just spent the last 2 chapters talking about how to accomplish what we want to accomplish", and I will agree with you. But what you have got to see is that it is about you designing your life. I am a firm believer about having our life by design instead of other things designing our lives for us. What I am trying to say is that when you enter a state of having a balanced lifestyle, the HOW you will accomplish your goal will be different than you expect.

For example, you might have mapped out to lose 50lbs and be in the best shape of your life. During this time, you also have a goal to make $10,000 more at the end of the year. What you will realize is that HOW you go about reaching those goals will be completely left to the grace of God. Each of us have desires. Things that we want in this life to happen for us. I am here as living proof that you can have what you want. The key is having a balanced lifestyle and when you do that, the thought of making $10,000 through selling shirts will take a turn and surprise you. Instead, it will be through someone at the gym noticing you, and then interviewing you on how you lost that weight, and then pay you $2000 for 5 speeches for them specifically wanting to know what you did to lose the weight. The key here to remember again that it does not matter how you get there, what matters is that you get there. So, remember you already have everything you want. You just have to make sure you have a balanced lifestyle and let life happen for you!

BONUS CHAPTER
What Really Matters

We have now come to a journey where you are an individual who has the necessary tools so that you can start living the life that you want. But before you do this you must think about what really matters to you. What is something that you want to do before you leave this planet?

Many times, we never get to reach this point in our life because we never take the initiative to take the steps necessary so that we can be free and not let things hold us back. I truly believe each and every one was made for a purpose. There is a reason why you love the things you do. In that I truly believe that there is something you can do to help complete what you love. Whether it is helping the homeless, or giving food to the needy because it is something you can relate to. We each have those things in the world that we want to be able to change. Some of us might not know exactly what it is or how to figure it out, but we know why we want to do it. The key to knowing what you enjoy always has to do with GIVING BACK.

A lot of times it might seem that what you are currently giving does not make a difference. But it is those little things that actually are the most important. Sometimes your giving does not have to be in an actual physical item. It can be that of time or knowledge. Realize the value of those little things and do them to the best of your ability. It is vital that you connect yourself to a cause in the world. When you are able to connect yourself to a cause in the world, you are able to give something to the people and to leave the world a better place. When you really take your mind off of yourself, you are able to focus onto what truly matters. No longer are you tied down by the bitterness or doubts that you face. No longer are you in a job that drains your energy. Your perspective in life has changed. There is nothing holding you back.

You have now come to realize what truly matters when you have taken the time to fix the problems that you have been carrying with you and dealing with your entire life. As you do these things, you start to feel a sense of completeness. I will never forget the moment when I helped a guy on the side of the street. That was a feeling I will never forget. Or, the time I helped provide food for a family that was in need. It was a feeling that is unexplainable and a feeling that everyone in the world should experience. It is at this very moment, that you have come to grips with yourself, the true feeling of what it means to live in this world. True living starts happening when you GIVE. Now besides giving you all of the knowledge that I have spent the last 33 years of my life learning, I would like to take some time and give you two more things that have helped me in my life. I refer to them as 2 of my sideline hustles.

1. How to practically accomplish anything you are trying to go after.

2. How to jump into the real estate investing world today!

Sideline Hustle 1: Accomplishing any of your goals!

I remember when I first started my business. After taking all the money I had saved, including my retirement and investing it in my business, after 11 months I still had not made any money. From driving all the way to Florida, to sleeping in a car in Dallas, in order to learn the business in real estate I was determined to make it. I was determined to run a successful business so that I could be financially free. After 5 years, I went from making no money for nearly a year, to being able to make a six-figure salary, purchase a house for myself, give my mom a house to stay in, and also give my wife the opportunity for her not to have to work anymore. I am here to tell you that you can do the exact same thing, as long as you follow these 3 simple steps.

Step 1: Consistency! Establish a morning routine. There are many days you will not feel like getting up. Something that kept me going was reading my affirmations, the priming in the morning, and also making sure I spent time with my God, and also planned my day, taking cold showers, exercising in the morning, and reading. The determination to want to master my morning routine allowed me to push through the days that I did not want to push through.

Step 2: Waking up early, and exercising. By making the decision to wake up early you already get a head start in the world. If you are someone who is up by 5am, you pretty much have a total of 3 hours every day, for the next 5-7 days is like 15 hours! I made the decision to get up at 3am every day, and work for about 6-7 days every week. This allowed me to get a total of 30 plus hours every week. This is what allowed me to take my real estate business to the next level.

Step 3: Create your goals, but make them practical, and look at them every single day and night before you go to bed. If you really want to lose weight, don't just say you want to lose 100lbs. By looking into it you will see that it is healthy to lose about 1-2lbs a week. Therefore, an actual goal would be to lose 75lbs.

Consistency, waking up early and creating goals each and every week-by doing these 3 things you will be able to accomplish any goal you put your mind to.

Now this is what I would like for you to do right now. Take out a notepad on your iPhone, or on your sketch pad. I would like for you to imagine the year 2021 and to think about what goals you would like to have accomplished by the end of the year. Ready, set go!

Sideline Hustle 2: Jumping into the real estate world today!
Okay, now that you got some of your goals written down, let me give you the knowledge on how to get started in real estate today!

Make the jump today and join the real estate investing world!

I will now explain to you how to invest in Real Estate with 0 money down. The only thing you need to remember is these 3 practical things.

In 2015, I had no idea about how to work in real estate. Nearly 5 years later, I have been able to conduct several transactions, and made more money than I ever thought I would make!

The 1st thing is to learn about real estate investing. There are a lot of books currently out there. The easiest thing to do is to go to your nearest library and look through all of the real estate investing books that exist.

After you find a couple, research who the authors are. Once you figure out who has the best review, read the book.

The 2nd thing to do is go to a real estate investment club. There are currently many investment clubs around the country. Many times, you have to pay to get in, but just by asking the person setting up the event, many times, they will allow you to sit in the first meeting for free. Believe it or not, you can even volunteer and assist the owner.

The 3rd thing to do is to find someone who is willing to mentor you, and show you the ropes. Many times, the real estate game is filled with so much knowledge, that it can take you months before you start understanding the way this profession is run. The best thing to do is to learn from the experts. Ask if there is anything you can do for them. Ask if you can shadow them. Even ask what books they recommend.

The big 3 is be willing to learn about real estate investing, surround yourself with real estate investors, and get coached by real estate investors. Everything you want you already have; you just have to be aware of it!

What I would like you to do now is to get on your phone, and look up your nearest real estate investing club. Figure out who the point of contact is and email them to set up a meeting.